55

'85

TESS

The Story of a Guide Dog

TESS
The Story of a Guide Dog

Photographs by

FAY GODWIN

Text by

PETER PURVES

LONDON
VICTOR GOLLANCZ LTD
1981

Text © Peter Purves 1981
Photographs © Fay Godwin 1981
ISBN 0 575 02959 5

Typeset by Rowland Phototypesetting Ltd
Bury St Edmunds, Suffolk and
printed in Spain by
Graficromo-SA, Cordoba

CONTENTS

Part One
Tess at Tollgate House   9

Part Two
Puppy-Walking
1:   Tess's New Home   27
2:   The First Lessons   43
3:   Tess on the Town   48

Part Three
Wokingham
1:   Re-assessment and Early Training   67
2:   Advanced Training   81
3:   Fulfilment   89

Epilogue   126
A Short History of the Guide Dog Movement   127

Our book is for all those who work with The Guide Dogs for the Blind Association; for Kathy and her "new pair of eyes"; and for the viewers of "Blue Peter" who over the years have given much-needed support to the Association.

Part One

Tess at Tollgate House

Tess was born at Tollgate House, near Leamington Spa, which since 1970 has been the breeding and puppy-walking centre of the Guide Dogs for the Blind Association. Surrounded by tall trees and sweeping lawns, the ivy-covered stucco house was built in the 1930s, probably as a wealthy family's retreat from the bustle of the nearby Midland towns, and the black notice with gold lettering at the entrance to the drive is the only indication of its present use from the road.

Behind the house, the work of the breeding centre is carried on in three low buildings and several acres of lovely Warwickshire countryside. On the right of the pathway leading to these buildings are some fenced open runs, each with its own entrance to the kennel block behind. This block is the home of the Association's stud dogs; they live there awaiting the arrival of the brood bitches, which are boarded out with private families and brought to the centre for mating and whelping.

As Derek Freeman, the puppy-walking and breeding manager of the GDBA, walked down the path one afternoon, he paused for a moment to look at a black labrador which was chewing contentedly on a bone in the centre of one of the runs.

"Hello there, Uffa," he said in his gentle Yorkshire accent. "Good boy, good boy."

Uffa at once dropped the bone and gave a protective growl.

"Now now, Uffa, that won't do," said Derek, opening the metal-mesh gate quickly and moving inside the enclosure with the dog, which now stood gently wagging its tail. As Derek approached, Uffa dropped his head to pick up the bone again.

"Leave it, Uffa. Leave."

He reached forward and took the bone without resistance from the labrador's mouth, and gently tapped him on the muzzle with it. Then, holding the bone just in front of the dog's mouth, Derek told Uffa again to "leave it". The dog obeyed. Derek pushed the bone at the dog's mouth but Uffa's jaws stayed firmly closed.

"Good boy, good boy," encouraged Derek, patting Uffa on the side, and then threw the bone down on the ground, where it stayed until Derek told Uffa to "take it". Uffa at once went and picked up the bone, and made no sound as Derek gave him a pat. Satisfied, Derek let himself out of the run.

Uffa's jaws remain firmly closed until the magic words: "Take it."

He continued his walk past several other runs where the occupants moved up to the fencing to exchange greetings with him. Over the years Derek had built up a relationship with every one of the animals in his care that many an owner of a single dog would envy. And his memory regarding each animal's history, temperament and breeding was like a catalogue.

At the end of the runs there is a covered arcade which divides the hospital block from the whelping block, and Derek entered the arcade and stopped in front of the glass-fronted door which marks the entrance to the whelping section. Then he changed his mind, turned and crossed the few yards to the hospital block. One of the kennel maids was there preparing something for a retired brood bitch which was in for treatment.

As Derek washed his hands at the sink he asked the girl: "Anne, has anyone had any trouble with Uffa?"

"No, I don't think so," answered Anne.

"I just wondered, because he growled at me as I talked to him—he had his bone. Mind, he's all right now, though."

10

"Well, he's always been lovely with me," said the girl.

"I didn't think it was anything to worry about—there's nothing on his card, I know that. But we'll keep an eye on him anyway."

Derek's concern was for the temperament of the pups Uffa would sire. He had been selected for stud because his breeding was exceptionally good: his mother had produced four litters of guide dog puppies, and there had been a very high success rate among them. Uffa should be an ideal sire, but if he had a protective streak, that would be something to be alert for in his litters. There must be no mistake when a puppy finally ends up with its blind owner. If his first litter produced that same streak, Uffa might not be used for stud again, at least not with the same bitch.

Always meticulous, Derek made a mental note to enter a query on the dog's card when he returned to his office, then dried his hands and left the room.

In the whelping block Ellen Harbourne, the kennel manager, was weighing a small bundle of curly black fur. Penny, a curly-coated black retriever, had produced a litter of ten pups two weeks earlier, and all the daily checks had to be carried out. The litter—four bitches and six dogs—was doing fine and although bitches are the preferred sex for guide dogs, all ten animals would be going on to the puppy-walking scheme when they were six weeks old.

Curly-coats are quite rare, and this was the first purebred litter to be produced at Tollgate House. Derek and his assistant Barrie Stocks had previously produced very successful crossbreeds in a beautiful "liver" colour, but Derek had wanted some pure breeding for a long time. He had collected the sire from Exeter some time before, and was delighted that the mating had produced such fine pups. Although she was still full of maternal protectiveness, Penny was quite content to allow Derek to approach her and the puppies. The day after they were born she had snapped at him when he approached her carelessly, but Derek would have been the first to admit that it was his own fault—the bitch didn't know him and he ought to have been much more circumspect.

There were nine pens in the whelping block, but only one other was currently in use, and that was the one where Harmony, a fine yellow labrador bitch, would soon have her litter. Harmony had been born at Tollgate House nine years earlier, one of only the second litter to be produced at the centre. All the brood bitches live with private families—invaluable voluntary helpers without whom the centre could not function—and they often whelp at their own homes, but Harmony had been brought back to Tollgate House nine days before, and her litter was due at any moment.

11

Harmony and Tango.

Harmony was out in her open run now, taking the air. She was in wonderful condition, her bulging tummy and pendulous dugs showing that she would shortly produce her sixth litter; because of her age, it would be her last one. She had been a highly successful bitch: just over 80% of her puppies had completed the training and qualified as guide dogs. It was a remarkable record—not the best ever recorded, because two brood bitches had managed a 100% success rate, but a record which suggested that this litter would be just as good. The pedigree and history of the sire, Tango, were also first class.

On being introduced to her whelping pen, Harmony had been given a heap of newspaper and wood-wool, and she had spent some time tearing them up and fashioning them into the nest in which she would whelp. Making that nest is a very important part of a bitch's preparations for giving birth, and Harmony kept rearranging it until it was perfect. She had always been a good mother, and no one at the centre expected her to have any trouble with her new litter.

In the corner of the pen, nearest to the metal-barred door, there was a large shelf raised some two feet from the floor, which would be Harmony's sanctuary from her pups when she needed some peace and quiet. After all, six weeks in the pen with anything up to ten pups could certainly put a great strain on any family relationship, however patient the mother! A bitch with her first litter has to be shown both what and where that sanctuary is, but the experienced Harmony would go straight to it as soon as she felt the need.

"Any problems, Ellen?" asked Derek.

"No. Penny and her lot are fine," Ellen replied. "I think Harmony may whelp tonight—before I let her out into her run she was having a right old go at the newspapers."

"Who's on evening duty tonight?"

"Judy, I think."

"Right," said Derek. "I'd better come and be with her tonight then, because I'm off to Marlborough to pick up an alsatian bitch tomorrow, and I won't be back until late. So if it doesn't happen tonight, you could be with her tomorrow."

The evening duty is the night watch from 8 p.m. Eighteen-year-old Judy had only been at one whelping before, and when the kennel girls are inexperienced Derek or Ellen always tries to be with them to supervise and instruct.

One of the resident cats has crept in to enjoy the warm nest, and the puppies get used to having cats around from the very earliest times.

"I'll be back at about five then," said Derek, and left the room as Ellen returned the pup she had been examining to the litter and took out the next one to complete her checks.

Derek came out into the open alongside the outdoor runs for the bitches in residence. In the first run, there were two yellow labradors and an alsatian, all between seven and nine months old; they were all on the puppy-walking scheme, and had been returned to Tollgate House while they were in season. These three came up to the bars to get a pat and a word of encouragement from Derek, and so did the two bitches in the second run. Harmony, in the third run, moved up to the gate slowly and heavily, her tail gently wagging.

"Hello, girl. Aren't you nice?" said Derek, touching her muzzle. "Yes, you're gorgeous."

Responding to the gentle tone of his voice, Harmony licked at his fingers as they rested on the bars of the gate.

"Oh yes, it could well be tonight," Derek thought as he went back to his office in the main house, with its large window overlooking the back lawn.

Meanwhile, Ellen had completed her examination of Penny and her brood. She opened the gate to Harmony's pen, checked that it was as clean as she had known it would be, and then she went to the back door of the block to admit the mother-to-be.

Derek Freeman and the rest of the team often handle the pups—this keeps them in constant touch with the pups' progress.

Harmony wandered over as soon as she was called, and followed the girl back to her pen. She climbed straight on to her nest, lifting herself heavily up the six inches or so of the raised area, and then flopped down in the corner. From then on Ellen and, later, Derek would be watching for any signs that the bitch was ready to produce the little yellow bundles that would be nurtured and cherished so that they would grow up fit and strong to join the ranks of the "eyes of the blind".

Most bitches tend to wait until the early evening, or at least the late afternoon, before whelping. It seems that they need the calm and quiet of that time, and it is rare for whelping to start during the middle of the day. Harmony was no exception.

When Derek relieved Ellen at ten to five, there had still been no sign from the bitch that she was even thinking about giving birth. She lay quietly in her corner, breathing evenly, and giving every indication that she was deeply asleep. Ellen said goodbye to Derek and left to collect one of the stud dogs, in her charge for the night: each of the kennel staff take one of the dogs into the house with them for the night, one of the ways which the dogs' temperament and character can be regularly observed.

Shortly after twenty past five, Derek saw Harmony come quite suddenly wide awake. She slowly rose and turned round, gave a slight whine, tried to

In the pen.

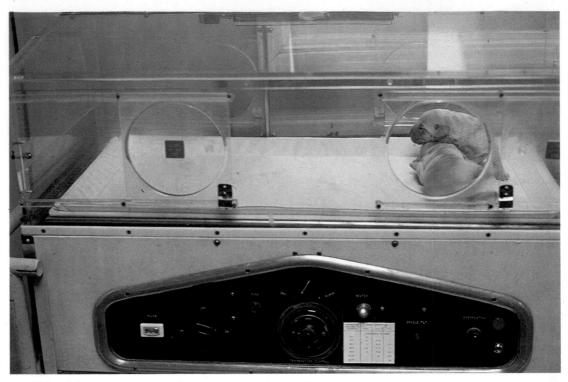

The first two pups are kept warm and out of the way while the rest of the litter is born.

settle again, and then heaved herself up on to all fours and moved over to a fresh clump of newspapers, at which she began to nuzzle. Then she settled in a prone position with her forelegs on the newspaper and began to tear at it. The activity became more determined as Derek watched, and he knew that Harmony could well be showing the first of the whelping symptoms. He immediately got up, crossed the small room and picked up the telephone to call the main building. He left a message there for Judy, telling her that she should join him in the whelping block, as it appeared that Harmony was about to start her labour.

By the time the girl arrived it was nearly six o'clock. Harmony had been very active in building yet more of the nest, and now she was panting quite heavily.

"Is this it?"

"Oh yes," said Derek. "She won't be long now. She started about half an hour ago, and with a bitch this experienced, it shouldn't take her long to get going."

Nor did it. Harmony looked deeply concerned as she scratched at her bed area, tore at the wadding and, as her panting continued, began to shiver. At that point her temperature was beginning to fall from its normal 101° to about 98° as a cooling preparation for the new pups: they were going to be very much cooler in the outside world than they had been in Harmony's womb.

Everything was ready for the whelping. A new extension with indoor runs had been added to the block a few years before, and there was a water supply connected to a hose for washing the pups and the mother as the whelping went ahead. The temperature in the block had now been raised to 70°, and the incubator had been switched on. There was a supply of milk and glucose to give Harmony every two hours or so.

Harmony was whining and crying quite a lot by now, and Derek and Judy calmly murmured gentle words of encouragement to her. Unless there were any signs of difficulty, neither would interfere. By half-past six, Harmony had gone into the second stage of labour, and the two observers saw the beginning of the contractions which would expel the first of her puppies. It didn't take long. Within ten minutes the first of the Guide Dogs for the Blind Association's "T" litter was pushed out into the world. There was nothing at all to teach Harmony. She quickly nuzzled her newborn pup, licking away the caul—rather like a polythene bag—before nipping through the umbilical

The puppies need constant feeding.

cord with her teeth, not too near the puppy's tummy, not too distant. Then, her exertion over, she cleaned herself and flopped her head down for a rest.

At once the two helpers moved into action, Derek supervising as Judy did the work for the first time. She took up the tiny wet bundle, calming the anxious bitch as she did so, dried it delicately with a warm towel, and popped it onto the scales, checking its sex—male—and looking to see if there were any abnormalities. Then she took the puppy back to Harmony and placed him on one of the huge nipples, where he immediately began sucking. It is most important that new-born puppies should want to feed, and Derek saw at once that this pup was all right—it was breathing properly and had no visible abnormalities. One down. How many to go?

The second pup, also a male, was born with no difficulty 45 minutes later, and both lay with their eyes tightly shut, sucking from Harmony. After the third birth, yet another male, Derek said, "That's Topper, Tweed and Tag so far. Let's hope that we get some females soon."

As was usual, the first-born was then taken from Harmony and placed in the incubator, which was provided some years ago with money raised by the

Pups are used to seeing cats from birth but it's still fun to investigate.

BBC children's television programme "Blue Peter". The third puppy was then put to suckle.

A good two hours had now passed since the bitch had begun to produce her pups, and Derek knew he would soon have to let Harmony out into her open run so that she could relieve herself. After letting her suckle the two pups for another ten minutes or so, Derek and Judy took them from her, popped them in the incubator, and persuaded Harmony to go to the door with Judy. The labrador still had that concerned frown around her eyes as she wandered out into the run. It was just after twenty to nine, and there was no moon as she moved away from the shaft of light thrown into the run by the open door and into the darkness.

"Shut the door and stay with her, Judy," said Derek. "Watch her all the time—you might think that she's straining to pass a motion when really she could drop another pup."

But there was no mishap outside, and shortly the two returned; Harmony went straight to her bed area, settling down heavily on her side. Tweed and Tag were then put back to her.

It's never too soon to think about the next meal.

Five minutes later, Harmony's fourth puppy—a bitch, Tara—was alive, well and being cleaned before being put back to suckle, with Tweed joining Topper in the incubator.

"How do you think she's doing?" asked Judy.

"Oh, this is marvellous," said Derek. "She's only been going a little over two and a half hours and already she's had four. If this keeps up she could break all her previous records."

"Shall I offer her some glucose and milk?"

"Yes, I think she could do with it."

But Harmony didn't break any records that night. After that initial burst, there was a long gap. If, as seemed most likely, there was a fifth pup, it didn't seem eager to join its brothers and sister out in the world. Ten o'clock passed, and half-past ten. Harmony showed no sign of urgency as she occasionally nuzzled the two pups she was suckling.

Then at ten minutes to eleven, with as little fuss as could be imagined, out popped number five. Another bitch. Tess.

Judy did the cleaning quickly and expertly now, but as she went to weigh the puppy, she suddenly stopped.

"It's not breathing, Mr Freeman!"

Young pups spend a good deal of their waking time playing.

22

"I'll do it," said Derek, quickly taking the tiny yellow puppy from the girl with both hands, enclosing its front legs. His thumbs firmly supported the nape of the neck, and his index fingers were curled under its chin to prevent the head from swinging. He moved over to the centre of the room, checking that there was nothing behind him, and stood with his feet about eighteen inches apart. Keeping his arms stiff, he vigorously swung the pup down between his legs five or six times, until no more fluid came from its mouth. Judy handed him a towel, and he dried the puppy carefully, massaging the body as he did so. The puppy began to struggle and cry loudly, and Derek immediately placed her on one of the nipples, where she began to suck at once.

The whole process had taken less than a minute and a half, and Tess had overcome the first hurdle of her very young life. Now she and Tara sucked from the contented Harmony while Tag joined his brothers in the incubator.

By one-thirty in the morning, Harmony had produced her sixth and final pup, another bitch, Tilly. It had been a good whelping—six puppies in seven hours, and apart from the alarm with Tess there had been no complications. Derek reflected that he was glad this hadn't been a "Z" litter; six names beginning with "Z" were hard to find! By two o'clock Harmony had been cleaned up, she had relieved herself outside, been given her drink, and she was bedded down with her youngsters. She would now nurse them for six weeks.

The puppies were inspected every day. Harmony fed them herself and although for 48 hours she was kept on a light diet, she was back to normal feeding after that. On the third day after the birth the vet came to look them over, and removed the dew claws from the puppies' legs. "T" litter proved to have no abnormalities, and all six puppies advanced at the correct rate. Tess was the last to open her eyes—a day after the others—but the daily checks showed that she was putting on weight properly and by the third week, when the kennel girls began to wean the pups from their mother's milk, there was little to differentiate them in size.

As the weaning progressed, the pups got more and more lively, and Harmony spent quite a lot of time away from them on her sanctuary in the corner. But she was a wonderful mum, keeping them all in order, nuzzling them away when they became too bothersome, and keeping them as clean as could be.

At five weeks old, the litter was a picture, and Derek said to Barrie Stocks, "I knew she'd produce some good ones. She always does. It's a shame it's her last litter— I don't want to lose this breeding line, so we'll keep an eye on the three bitches with a view to keeping one of them back as a brood bitch."

23

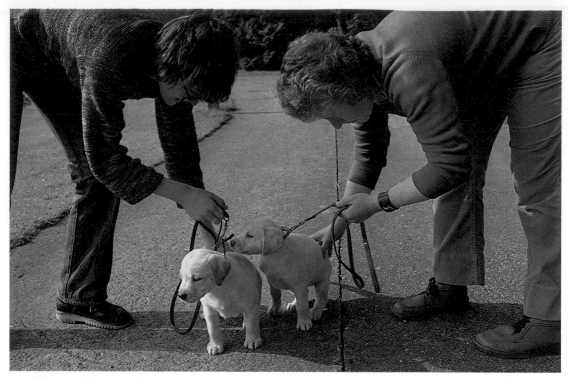

Time to be introduced to collar and lead just before leaving Tollgate.

Not fleas, but a curiously new sensation.

Derek Freeman fires a pistol to check a pup's reactions.

Six weeks and a day after being born, the puppies were finally separated from Harmony, who went back to her home and retirement. The pups were beginning to show one or two differences in temperament. Topper and Tweed were by far the most confident, and nothing at all bothered them. As they rolled about on the grass one day, Derek fired a starting pistol near them, but they totally ignored it. Derek was able to observe that there was no adverse reaction to the noise from any of the pups—apart from Tess.

The puppies were carefully observed at feeding time and at play, and Derek and his staff gleaned a great deal from what they saw. Tess appeared just a little bit sensitive—not nervous, but certainly very much aware of what was going on around her. Derek decided that she would have to go to an experienced puppy-walker because her sensitivity, if handled wrongly, could turn into a neurosis which would make her a failure as a guide dog.

By the time Harmony left for home, Derek had decided who would look after Tess for the next nine months. Edith Washington and her family had already walked three dogs on the scheme, and in two days' time they would be returning a ten-month-old labrador to Tollgate House for its final assessment; it would then be allocated to one of the main guide dog training centres. A month before, Edith had said she would be delighted to walk another labrador. Her first two puppies had both qualified as guide dogs and, according to the supervisor's reports, the progress of the puppy the Washingtons were about to return had been excellent. If Tess needed careful and experienced handling, the family would fit the bill.

This is not to say that Tess wasn't a perfectly good puppy, but as training a guide dog is an expensive business, everything possible is done to ensure success. And in the initial stages, the choice of the puppy-walker is absolutely crucial.

Two days before going to their new homes, the puppies were given their first distemper injections and a vaccination against parvovirus, a virus which is thought to be a mutation from feline enteritis and which attacks fast-growing tissue in puppies; as it is a killer, this protection is absolutely essential.

When they were just six and a half weeks old, "T" litter left Tollgate House in special travelling boxes in the backs of the vehicles which were to take them to their new homes in Wolverhampton, Nuneaton, Leamington and Warwick, and little Tess was off to meet the Washingtons of Southam.

Part Two
Puppy~Walking

CHAPTER ONE: Tess's New Home

THE PUPPY-WALKING scheme was the brainchild of N. M. (Callum) McLean, who in 1956, having seen the way guide dogs were trained in the United States, decided that if the British Guide Dog Association was to increase the supply of qualified dogs for the blind, it would have to take responsibility for their early training. He also had the foresight to realise that if the training centres then in operation at Exeter and Leamington were to receive a regular supply of suitable animals, the GDBA would have to set up its own breeding scheme.

When Derek Freeman joined the Association in 1959, the puppy-walking scheme was run from Leamington, and most of the dogs received for training were donated by well-wishers. Only 30% of the animals qualified at the end of training, and although this was not as unsatisfactory as might appear because the puppy-walking scheme was still in its infancy, it was obvious that a 70% failure rate could not be allowed to continue. It required some drastic new thinking for the Association to be able to stop accepting "cast-offs", and it fell to Derek to upgrade the fragmented methods then in use and get the breeding scheme under way. Finding dogs that would make good sires to selected bitches was an expensive undertaking, and the fact that the Association has realised its objective so successfully says much for the devotion of all its members and supporters to the task of fund-raising, and not least to the wide publicity given to the Association by the BBC children's television programme "Blue Peter"

The Association had neither the time nor the manpower to cope with the basic training of the large number of pups which were now becoming available, and house-training and early lessons in obedience were things that could be handled by non-professionals. So the puppy-walking scheme was set up, with the young pups being cared for in private homes within a 40-mile radius of the breeding centres from the time they were about six weeks old until, at approximately ten months of age, they could begin the intensive training which would transform them into fully fledged guide dogs.

Since 1959, thousands of puppies have passed through the Association's breeding, walking and training programmes, and the success rate for puppies in training is now almost 80%. At any one time, there are now over

27

500 puppies being reared at the Association's breeding centres in England and Scotland; there are 25 stud dogs living at the centres and 120 brood bitches being cared for in private homes. The five training centres at Exeter, Leamington, Wokingham, Bolton and Forfar produce approximately 430 qualified guide dogs each year. This is a wonderful record, but the work needs to grow even further, for even now only a small proportion of the blind people in the United Kingdom have the advantage of a well-trained dog to help them.

The day Tess left Tollgate House, Alison Wallis, the area supervisor, was delivering three puppies to their new homes.

First of all, Topper was taken to a small terraced house in the centre of Leamington Spa. The family were new to the scheme, and had written to the Association some months before asking if they could become puppy-walkers; they had been vetted by the Association and found to be suitable. Both the husband and wife were schoolteachers, though the wife had not worked since the birth of their children, now aged seven and five. Topper had shown himself already to be a dog of character and confidence, and a home in a busy town would not upset him, while the inexperience of the new walkers would be offset by the young puppy's willingness to learn.

There had been only one hold-up before the family were allowed a puppy to walk, and that had been because their small garden had a tumbledown fence leading onto a back alley; that had to be made secure before a puppy could live there. So much money is involved in training a puppy that there have to be as few opportunities as possible for one to go missing. Since 1960, out of the many thousands of puppies passing through the scheme, only eleven have been lost or killed, and only one of these was lost without trace, a record which shows the highest level of care.

Topper was handed over to his new owners with as little ceremony as possible—it was important that he should quickly feel secure in his new environment, and the sooner the family got to know him without distractions the better. They were given a leash, a collar and some grooming equipment, together with a medallion showing that the puppy was a trainee guide dog. Most important of all, there was a booklet containing advice on the care and welfare of their new charge. The supervisor would visit them every month, but it was up to them to get the puppy fully house-trained and teach him to walk well on a leash. They would have to make sure Topper was confident in a variety of different environments so that when he was ten months old he would be ready for the specialised training which would later qualify him to join the ranks of the "seeing eyes".

28

"Where am I?"

Tess and Tara were quiet and calm in their travelling boxes as Alison drove the Association's van out of Leamington Spa and along the A425 through the lovely Warwickshire countryside to the little market town of Southam. Although busy town settings are usually preferred for puppy-walking, Derek Freeman had felt that a more countrified environment would be better for the sensitive little Tess. Not that Southam, seven miles from Tollgate House as the crow flies, is always quiet—on market days it is full of activity, and as the main Warwick-Northampton road passes through the middle of the town there would be no shortage of traffic to give Tess experience when she was ready.

The puppies couldn't see out of the van as they passed the shops and buildings which Tess would get to know during the next few months—Simpson's the greengrocer's, the bread shop, the flower shop, the fish-and-chip shop next to Rockingham Motor Cycles, and the many pubs which include the fourteenth-century inn, the Old Mint, selling Sam Smith's Ale on draught. If Tess was to make the grade, all these places would have to become

29

familiar to her, causing her neither excitement nor concern. Fully trained guide dogs must ignore the smells and distractions of a town. As she steered the van out of the main street and along a side turning, Alison reflected on how rewarding her job was. She and her two colleagues, Marion Broughall and Diane Mawby, shared the work of supervising a wide area around the Tollgate centre, making monthly visits to all the walkers on the scheme. Each supervisor was devoted to the puppies in her care, and Alison knew she would soon get to know the untrained puppy she was about to deliver to the Washington's home.

Edith Washington lived with her husband Ken, who worked in a bank, their thirteen-year-old daughter Lisa and their son Matthew, who was eleven, on a modern estate about half a mile from the centre of Southam. It was a quiet road with well-kept gardens, and number 59 was much like its neighbours, a compact house built in the 1960s and looking bright and new because Ken had repainted the doors and windows the previous year. Alison knew it well, having visited Edith once a month for more than two and a half years, ever since the Washingtons joined the puppy-walking scheme.

As well as delivering the new puppy, Alison had to collect Melody, a ten-month-old labrador bitch the Washingtons had been walking for the last six months. Edith had been asked to take on Melody because she was an experienced puppy-walker. There had been a sudden illness in the family with whom Melody had been living, and they had not been able to devote the necessary time and energy to the puppy. Melody had progressed very well since then, and this was much to the credit of Edith Washington and Alison Wallis, who was now carrying Tess under her arm to the front door of number 59.

Edith was in the kitchen when the doorbell rang. Melody, lying in the corner, immediately gave a little bark and ran out into the hall, tail wagging furiously. Tess had just registered the dog's shape through the rippled glass when Edith opened the door.

"Hello Alison, I was expecting you. Come in." For a moment Melody prevented this from happening as she jumped up at Alison, but when the supervisor said firmly "No, girl," she sat back and looked faintly surprised as she registered the presence of the puppy the visitor was carrying. Tess attempted to keep the big dog in sight as Alison followed Edith into the living room.

This was a comfortable room with a low sofa, an easy-chair, a couple of occasional tables, a bookcase near the back wall, and a television set by the front picture window, on top of which were proudly displayed the two framed photographs presented to Edith by the Association showing the two

Alison carries Tess into her new home—

where she takes up a safe position to survey the scene.

qualified guide dogs she had walked as puppies. On the tables were vases of daffodils and yellow forsythia.

Alison put the puppy down on the light cord carpet, where Tess sat to take in her surroundings. Melody came straight over to investigate. A sniff, a whimper of delight, and Melody dropped down on her front legs, her rump high in the air and her tail lashing from side to side, inviting the youngster to play. When she was on her leash Melody knew she was working, and then she would have ignored any other dog, but here at home it was different.

As Tess backed away from this overbearing presence, Melody bounded at her, knocking her over.

"Gently, Mel, gently," warned Edith.

Tess tried to move again, and the bigger dog nuzzled at her, pushing her backwards. One or two collisions occurred before Tess found sanctuary beneath the sofa. There she lay, not cowed or frightened but safe and alert. Melody tried to get to her: time was when she too would have used the sofa as her sanctuary, but at ten months not even her head would fit underneath it.

When a changeover takes place the new pup is introduced before the departure of the older dog. It helps the newcomer to settle. But within the hour Melody would be leaving the Washingtons' house, and she would no longer be classed by the Association as a puppy but as an adult bitch in training.

Edith was thrilled with Tess. She would gladly have had half a dozen puppies at the same time if that had been allowed, and although she knew she would shed a few tears over Melody's departure, the new puppy would be a welcome challenge. It was hard to devote time and energy to bringing up a puppy which, when all the work was done, would be taken away from you. But like all dedicated puppy-walkers, Edith could accept this philosophically and carry on with training the next one. She tried not to get too devoted to the puppies she cared for, but in the end she always came to love each one as if it were her own, and wept when the time came for them to go. Today would be no exception.

Alison stayed for a good half hour, chatting about Melody and reminding Edith about feeding young pups, but as Edith had been through all this before there was very little to discuss. In the meantime, Tess had become bolder. She tried getting out from under the sofa three times, only to stop as Melody pushed her muzzle down at her. Melody got quite excited and jumped up onto the sofa, to be told "Come off!" by Edith: she obeyed at once. In that moment, Tess made her break. She crawled out from the back of the sofa and made a dash across the room, getting behind one of the small tables a split second before Melody's paw landed just where she had been. The

32

Melody keeps an eye on Tess as she explores the garden and tries to make contact with the family guinea-pig.

puppy sat still and looked around her; she was ready to explore, and Edith called Melody to her and made her sit.

Tess went "walkabout" as the two women carried on talking. Alison mentioned the puppy's sensitivity, and suggested that Edith wait a little longer than usual before introducing Tess to heavy traffic. There was no sign of nervousness as Tess explored the room, but as she approached Melody, the bigger dog could resist no longer, and jumped on her. The puppy struggled over onto her back, and lay there as Melody clambered all over her, and at one stage Tess managed to get into a sitting position under the big dog's tummy as though she was sheltering from the rain under a tent. Then they were both off again, Tess occasionally being flattened in the boisterous play.

There was no danger to the puppy, or the two women would have intervened; it was obvious that Tess was having fun. But in the middle of the game, Tess suddenly stopped and looked confused; the apparent smile on her face vanished for a second, and she made to squat down. Edith was there in a flash. She scooped the puppy from the floor under the nose of the

Closer investigation of the decor.

34

inquisitive Melody and whisked her out through the kitchen and into the garden.

The garden was about 35 feet long, and almost square. There were strong lattice fences on each side of it, with narrow, soil-filled borders to what had been a fine healthy lawn some years before. It still bore traces of grass, but was mostly a well-worn patch of earth with occasional holes, bearing witness to the labradors' inbuilt lack of "green fingers". You can't keep young puppies and gardens in order at the same time.

Edith put the puppy on one of the small patches of grass in the corner saying, "Busy girl, busy". Edith had shown her experience, not only in spotting that Tess needed to "perform" but in using the training word "busy" at the very first opportunity. All guide dog puppies are trained to relieve themselves to this command, and although Tess was not aware of it she had already been given her first lesson. As the puppy finished, Edith said "Good girl, good girl," and Tess responded by bounding over to her, obviously enjoying the praise. In time she would associate the words and actions together.

"I don't think you're going to have any trouble with her, do you?" asked Alison when Edith brought the puppy back into the house.

"No, I don't think so," replied Edith. "She really is lovely."

"Right, well I'll just get Mel, and then I'd better go. I've still got another one to deliver, and one more to collect. Oh, by the way, don't forget to worm her in nine days will you. I'll be back in four weeks to see how you're getting on."

Melody was delighted when Alison attached her lead. Edith felt a twinge of emotion as the labrador led Alison to the door. She loved Melody, and wouldn't see her again after today. Looking at the young puppy in her arms, she wondered if she would ever feel the same about Tess.

"Silly ass," she thought. "Of course I will." Cheering up, she shut the puppy in the living room and followed Alison and Melody down the front path to the van.

Alison put Melody in the back and got into the driving seat. The two women exchanged goodbyes, and Edith watched sadly as Alison drove away. As the van disappeared from view, she turned quickly back to the house before bursting into tears.

Meanwhile, Tess was finding her new surroundings most interesting. She hadn't been unhappy on her own, and had spent a minute or two re-exploring the area around which Melody had chased her. She jumped up at one of the tables, just hard enough to dislodge the vase of forsythia twigs with their yellow flowers. The vase hadn't broken, but the water had trickled down over the edge, making a little puddle on the carpet, and a couple of

the twigs had reached ground level. Tess was discovering how nice they were to chew when Edith came back into the room.

"Oh no, Tess, no. You bad dog. No," she said firmly, at once forgetting everything except the mild destruction in the corner of her living room. The puppy ignored her and continued to chew as Edith approached.

"No, Tess, no," Edith repeated, reaching down to give her a little light smack, at the same time taking the twigs from her.

Tess registered the gesture and the firmness in Edith's tone, and sat still to watch. This concentration lasted all of a split second before the puppy was off again in search of something else to play with.

Edith straightened the table, took the vase and the flower remnants through to the kitchen and brought back a cloth to clean up the mess. Tess thought this was all done for her benefit. She gambolled over to Edith, who was now kneeling down to dry up the puddle, and grabbed the flapping end of the cloth. A playful tug-of-war took place, and Edith found that she instantly liked this new puppy, despite its rather destructive conduct. "You've certainly got spirit, Tess," she thought.

Young puppies spend a great deal of time asleep, and Tess was no exception. The little game tired her and she looked ready for a rest. Edith had

prepared a large cardboard box with one side cut away and an old blanket in the bottom of it, and placed it in the corner of the kitchen away from any draughts. She took the puppy into the garden for another "busy" session, and when Tess promptly relieved herself Edith praised her profusely.

Praise following a puppy's doing anything correctly is an essential part of the training of any dog. The animals soon realise that a correct response on their part brings them pleasure, and this is part of their conditioning to words of command. "Busy" is the word used by all trainers, instructors and puppy-walkers in the Guide Dogs for the Blind Association, and in fact most of the training commands are standardised. This is done so that anyone taking over an animal during its training can get the correct response. Other commands, like "down", "sit", "stay", "leave", "wait" and "come" are self-explanatory. It would be some time before Tess was responding correctly to all of them, because she would only learn to concentrate sufficiently when she got older.

Edith brought Tess back into the kitchen and put her in her bed-box.

"There you are Tess. On your bed," she said.

Tess sat up, looked at Edith, turned round and sniffed at the old blanket, then half stepped and half tumbled out of the open side of the box.

"No, Tess. On your bed," repeated Edith, picking up the puppy and putting her back in the box. The phrase and action were repeated three times more before the puppy got the message, lay down, closed her eyes and was almost instantly asleep. With a bit of luck, Edith would now have time to finish making the beds—a job she was just about to do when Tess had arrived that morning.

Tess digs her heels in the first time Matthew takes her for a walk.

Tess slept for about three-quarters of an hour, and awoke at the same time that Matthew Washington got home from school for lunch. His school was only a stone's throw away, and Matthew had run home as fast as he could in the hope that he would not miss the new puppy's arrival.

"I'm home Mum," he called after opening the front door with the key that Edith made him carry on a string around his neck—he had a bad habit of losing things. "Has it arrived yet . . .?" His voice tailed off as he came into the kitchen in time to see Tess making her first movements to get out her bed. "Oh it's sweet," he continued. "What's its name?"

"It's a 'she' and she's called Tess," replied his mother. "I'm just getting her food ready, but she'll have to go out in the garden first."

The family would have to ensure Tess did this every time she awoke from a sleep, at least whilst she was still very young. From a practical point of view, the more opportunity she was given to go outside, the less chance there would be of her disgracing herself on the carpet. As Edith brought Tess back into the house, she heard the front door, and her daughter Lisa called out: "It's all right Mum; it's only me."

"Lisa, what on earth are you doing home? What about school dinner?"

"I just wanted to see the puppy—I'm going straight back after I've seen her," she said breathlessly.

Matthew and Lisa watched as the puppy attacked her lunch of a little raw meat chopped up very fine with some suet and brown bread, and after many "ooh's" and "ah's", Lisa was chivvied back to school and Matthew and his mother sat down to eat their scrambled eggs on toast. They decided to have it on their laps in the living room, and were sitting on the sofa when Tess came into the room.

She had a look around, wandered to the front of the sofa, and then, without a warning, leaped up at Matthew's knee. The boy was just a whisker too slow—one paw went into the scrambled egg, spraying his school jersey with the mushy mixture. Tess registered surprise at the brief panic that ensued as she trailed bits of egg around the room to shouts of "Tess, no", and "Tess come".

"I don't know about being sensitive, but you're certainly clumsy," thought Edith as she watched the puppy in the garden a little later. Matthew had gone back to school, and Tess had had a thorough look round the ground floor—Edith was forever finding her under her feet, and the dog was very responsive to her voice. Tess had a look at the stairs and decided not to attempt them—Edith would let her try them when she was ready, because a young puppy can easily come to grief on a staircase the first time. When Edith went upstairs Tess whined until she came back into view, but then the puppy got a fright because as Edith came down it must have seemed to Tess that a giant was bearing down on her from above, and she shot into the living room and under the sofa. As Edith came in Tess emerged at once and bounded over to greet her.

Edith decided to go straight back upstairs and let the puppy see her come down again. She spoke to Tess all the time and this time the puppy just stood and wagged her tail.

"There's a brave girl, Tess," she said, and Tess wagged her tail even more furiously in response to a new "game". "You see, Tess, there's nothing to be frightened of, is there? What a good girl."

Edith was delighted to find that in that first day she had made real contact with the pup. Tess had a lot of character, and if things alarmed her at first she could take them in her stride the very next time she was in the same situation, much as Edith herself had been when she first began puppy-walking.

A few years earlier, Edith had felt the need to get out and about, but with the children so much younger it was difficult for her to take a job. Now she felt she had found an ideal solution. It was unpaid work—apart from the 25 pence a day towards the feeding costs—but Edith felt she was doing something really worthwhile. The first puppy, a labrador bitch called Zoë, was very hard work, but then everything had been new to her. When Alison had asked her if she wanted another puppy she had answered "yes" without a moment's hesitation. The day she returned her second puppy to Tollgate House she heard that Zoë had qualified and was now a working guide dog, and that justified all her efforts.

After the second puppy was returned there had been a gap in the puppy-walking as Ken Washington had been ill for some months, but as soon as he was fit again Edith contacted the centre. This time Alison asked her if she would take on a puppy which had been slightly neglected and needed a firm hand. That was Melody, and Edith had saved her from failure. She found her work more and more rewarding.

When the children came home from school they were delighted to be able to play with Tess and they struck up an immediate friendship; it was important for the pup to get to know them too.

Travelling back to Southam on the Midland Red Service bus that evening, Ken Washington was also looking forward to meeting the new labrador. He worked at the National Westminster Bank in Leamington Spa. The bank is about a hundred yards from the Pump Room, and overlooks a grassy park with the river running through it. There has been a guide dogs' training centre in Leamington for many years, and the instructors regularly use the centre of the town for teaching the animals how to deal with traffic. It had

41

been watching them that had made Ken suggest the idea of puppy-walking to Edith, and he had never regretted it—even though he was forever brushing yellow labrador hairs off his dark suits. It gave him great pleasure that Edith enjoyed looking after the puppies so much, and he was glad that his children were growing up in an atmosphere where kindness to animals and caring for them was important. Although he would have hated to be described as an "animal lover" because the phrase suggested soppiness to him, he was happy to help with the puppies in any ways he could. He also enjoyed talking to his friends and clients about them, and there was a cheerful camaraderie among the puppy-walking fraternity in the town.

Ken gave Edith a little hug as she took his coat from him, and he went into the kitchen to inspect the new arrival.

That evening, the puppy was the single most important thing in the Washington household. The family laughed as she investigated everything in reach. The children played with her with a tightly-knotted scarf, and they all took turns at seeing that she was "busy" outside. She had eaten her Weetabix, baby milk and gravy at five o'clock and, at nine, a little chopped meat and liver. She would have four small meals a day for the first few weeks of her stay in Southam.

After the children were bundled off to bed, Ken and Edith thought of watching TV before turning in. But they found Tess so interesting that by eleven they had seen nothing but the puppy's antics!

Ken took Tess into the garden for the last time that night, and then Edith put her into her bed-box. The kitchen door was closed and the light turned off. Tess was now on her own. It wasn't long before Ken and Edith heard the pup crying for company. But painful as it was to hear the plaintive wailing from downstairs, Edith knew better than to go to comfort her. Tess would have to learn to spend her nights alone, and the sooner she learned the better. But her distress was understandable. The previous night she had been one of a litter of eight puppies, all piled up and sleeping together. Tonight she was all on her own in a strange house, with no company at all. For an hour, as the rest of the household slept, the only sound from number 59 was that of a bewildered, tired and lonely puppy, crying in the dark.

But soon that noise stopped too, as little Tess went to sleep.

CHAPTER TWO: The First Lessons

WHEN EDITH WENT into the kitchen the next morning, she discovered that Tess had made a puddle on the linoleum floor. The puppy was unaware of her "crime" and Edith didn't scold her. Instead she greeted Tess, who was so obviously delighted to be out of "solitary", and then popped her out into the garden. There was no other sign of damage. Tess had obviously played with her rubber toys and had not been bored—her bed-box was still intact and she hadn't worried her blanket. These were good signs that she would settle down easily.

Edith brought her back into the house, and was laying the table for breakfast when Lisa, dressed in her blue school uniform, came downstairs.

"Can I feed Tess, Mum?" she asked.

"Yes, love. Give her some Farex with this milk I'm heating. Beat an egg in it too, if you like."

Lisa set about preparing the food. Breakfast was the one meal the puppy would have at the same time as the rest of the household. Tess would have to learn that generally she did not eat at the same time as the humans. This would stop her wanting scraps from the table.

As Tess demolished her bowl of cereal, Ken and Matthew came down.

"Did she wet the floor, Mum?" asked the boy, with the air of someone who already knew what the answer would be. "I thought she would."

Before the breakfast party broke up Matthew helped by taking Tess out into the garden again.

"Right, upstairs, and do your teeth, and wash your hands again, Matthew—you've been playing with the puppy," said Edith as they returned.

Tess was quite absorbed in watching the bustle of the family starting their day. She sat at the bottom of the stairs without alarm as the humans went up and down. Ken was the first one away to catch his bus, and then the children. Tess became adventurous enough to climb up onto the first of the stairs, and as Matthew clattered past her, she turned and fell off.

"Silly dog, Tess," he said, giving her a pat, and was gone.

At last there was quiet again at number 59.

Edith realised that the staircase was quite a big obstacle for Tess, and she shut the puppy in the living room when she went upstairs to tidy the bedrooms. After a moment she heard the pup whining for her, and she got a tremendous welcome when she returned to her.

"What shall we do today?" asked Edith, already deciding that as the weather was dry and clear, she would take her new charge out straightaway. Before Alison's next visit, she would have to get through a lot of hard work with the puppy, and, bearing in mind the warning about her sensitivity, Edith decided that she would not venture into the heart of the town until Tess had begun to show a degree of confidence in her. She put the tiny collar with the medallion round the puppy's neck, checking that she could easily get a couple of fingers under the collar without choking her, and then attached the lead and took Tess out through the front door.

Tess didn't like the lead at all and just sat down on the front path. Edith didn't try to drag her along, but stepped back towards her to release the tension on the lead. "Come on, silly girl," she said cheerfully, but Tess stayed put as the lead became taut.

Once again Edith tried to coax the puppy forward without success. She had experienced this trouble with puppies before, and so she picked Tess up and carried her to the main footpath. Tess was not showing any signs of anxiety— no shivering or panting—and Edith knew it would only be a matter of days before the pup got used to the lead and was raring to go, but at the moment she was just raring to stay where she was. Edith tried a different tack, by turning to go in the opposite direction, and Tess stood up until the lead tightened, whereupon she sat down again. Round again went Edith, talking to Tess the whole time, and eventually, the pup decided that sitting still wasn't much fun, and at last set off along the path.

Suddenly there were lots of new things to see and to smell, and the world became very interesting. The road was quiet, with no traffic except for an electric milk-float which purred its way down the slight incline, receiving hardly a glance from the little puppy. They went down an alley between two houses which led them into a grassy field, in the corner of which was a small children's playground. A mother was giving her twins a swing, and another was slowly pushing her infant on the roundabout.

"It's never too early to socialise with children," thought Edith, and led the puppy over towards them. On the way, Tess stopped to relieve herself on the grass, and Edith made the mental note that Tess liked grass as her "toilet" and that she must make sure to train her to respond to the word "busy" on any surface. It would be awful if Tess would only use grass, and her blind owner lived in a concrete jungle!

The twins ran to greet the puppy. Some dogs can get quite alarmed at the unpredictable movements of young children, and guide dogs must take it all in their stride. Tess did. She showed her delight by jumping up and wagging

44

at everything in sight, and both Edith and the children's mother had to keep their respective charges under control.

Tess was so interested in what was going on that Edith lifted her onto the roundabout and, with one hand guarding the puppy, pushed it into motion. Tess thought this was wonderful, and was full of interest in the toddler on the other side who was straining to watch her.

Then Edith lifted her down and when they reached the middle of the field she unfastened the lead, leaving the puppy free to romp about. Tess had to jump quite high to clear the tufts of grass, and she raced back and forth. She discovered Edith's shoelaces, and managed to undo one of them as they played. Then Edith ran a little way off and called the puppy to her. Tess responded by charging back to her side. This was very good: although it was only a game, Tess had obeyed when she was called.

When it was time to go, Edith refastened the leash before opening the gate, but as Tess went straight under the gate there was a tangle of lead, puppy and handler which took a while to sort out. Taking every opportunity of introducing some training, Edith calmed the puppy and made her sit while she undid

Lisa feeding Tess—she will often hand-feed the puppy so that Tess will never react angrily if her food is taken away.

the clasp on the gate, and then she encouraged Tess to walk through with her. Again, there was much praise for the successfully completed sequence. Over the next weeks, all these actions would have to be repeated time and time again, and there would be many failures. But Edith had patience.

They continued their walk past Matthew's school. Some thirty ten-year-olds were playing a game of ball and skittles in the playground, and Tess took an immediate interest. She was quite absorbed in the noise and movement when the ball clattered into the mesh fence about a yard behind her. She turned sharply to see where the noise had come from, but after a reassuring word from Edith she carried on trotting along the footpath.

Back at the house, Edith got Matthew's lunch and made a pie for the evening meal, as well as preparing some chopped meat for Tess, who was now asleep. Then she collected some more puppy toys from the cupboard—a rubber ring, a short length of knotted rope and an old glove—which she put in the corner by the bed-box. Tess would soon find them and Edith knew that the more toys the puppy had to play with, the less chance there would be of her destroying anything valuable; she well remembered Melody eating a brand-new book the day after she had been allowed to tear up an old newspaper!

In the afternoon they had another walk along the paths near the house. That meant Tess couldn't be off her leash at all, but it was all good practice. Two children on bicycles stopped to chat with Tess, and so did one or two dogs and their owners. The puppy was interested in them all, but Edith kept her away from a rather mangy mongrel out for a stroll on its own. Tess didn't seem reluctant to meet people or animals, and the few cars in the quiet roads caused her no concern.

The family again spent the evening playing with Tess, and when they all settled down for the night, the puppy could be heard whining and yelping on her own in the kitchen. But eventually she was quiet and Edith, who had lain awake listening, breathed a sigh of relief and turned over to go to sleep.

During that first week, Edith and Tess visited the playground again, and tangled themselves up in the gate a couple of times; met babies in pushchairs; watched a coal delivery from a big truck; often passed the children in the school playground, where Tess recognised Matthew through the fence; and saw several cats at a distance and dogs at close quarters. Edith learned a lot about her new puppy. Tess was fairly responsive to her voice, and voice control was going to be a very important part of the dog's training as she got older. Tess still preferred grass to any other surface for her natural functions, but Edith had persuaded her to use the gutter on a couple of occasions. Tess's friendliness with strangers was also a good sign, and though there was still a problem with the lead at the beginning of her walks, it was early days yet.

"I think that tomorrow I'm going to take you into the main street," said Edith to the puppy as she put her to bed on the Friday night. "It's high time you had a bit of noise around you." Then she switched off the light, shut the door, and was relieved when the whimpering lasted for no more than a couple of minutes.

There is never more than one puppy in a family, so that during the most formative time it has as much human companionship as a normal family pet.

CHAPTER THREE: Tess on the Town

MATTHEW AND LISA played with Tess every night. Tug-o'-war with the knotted scarf was the labrador's favourite game, and one of which the children tired long before the puppy. Play is an important part of training, and is encouraged by the Guide Dogs for the Blind Association because so much can be done while a puppy is having a good time. The word "leave" meant nothing to Tess yet, but occasionally she would stop tugging and chewing, and was surprised to be praised. Edith had to use the word a lot, for the pup often picked up small stones and objects which she could easily have swallowed. Puppies quite often have to have treatment to remove foreign bodies from their throats and stomachs. That was one reason why Edith never let Tess play with a ball: small hard rubber ones can easily block a young pup's breathing, and bursting tennis balls lodged in the throat had been very nearly fatal to a couple of animals on the scheme. Sticks were "out" too—there is at least one recorded death of a puppy through impaling itself and piercing its windpipe. Edith usually found a good solid chunk of wood for Tess to play with in the field.

Edith thought it was now time one of the children took Tess for her morning walk, and so on the Saturday she told Matthew he could have the first turn—Lisa was playing netball for her school. On went the pup's collar and the lead was attached, but Matthew found it very hard going. Tess dug in her heels at the front door and it took nearly five minutes for the two of them to reach the main footpath a few yards away. But at last they set off and when they came back from the field Matthew was full of praise for the puppy's behaviour.

At about two o'clock Edith decided to go into the town. The main street of Southam is about a quarter of a mile long, and carries quite a lot of traffic, but most heavy trucks are off the road on a Saturday afternoon and the street was fairly quiet as Edith and Tess set off down the hill towards the shops. Guide dogs are trained to walk on the left side of the handler, and that meant that as they walked, Tess was nearer to the traffic than Edith. With a bolder puppy this would have been all right, but Tess's tail dropped and she tried to edge to the inside of the pavement. So Edith picked her up and carried her to the opposite pavement where, with Edith now between the puppy and the traffic, they set off again.

48

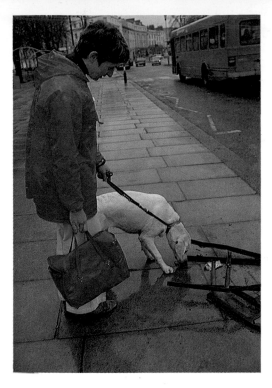

At this early stage Tess is allowed to investigate unfamiliar objects, but later will be thoroughly trained not to be distracted by sights or smells.

At once Tess had more confidence and tried to rush off down the street. The sharp tug administered to the leash prevented this, and for a second or two Tess walked without pulling at all. But she soon forgot and set off at a sharper pace. Another tug; another few seconds of calmer walking; then she was off again. In the weeks to come, Tess would learn the correct way to walk on the lead. All her natural tendencies to pull to the side and be distracted would have to be painstakingly corrected. She would have to learn not to get under her handler's feet, which was precisely what she did as another dog and its owner met them. Edith untangled herself from puppy and lead and let Tess socialise briefly with the well-groomed spaniel.

All this time cars had been passing by on the main road, and Tess had ignored them all. After her initial fear, Tess took the town centre in her stride. Half-way down the road a large motorcycle was kicked into life by one of a group of leather-jacketed enthusiasts outside the specialist shop. Tess was initially startled by the din, but as Edith patted her and reassured her the puppy shrugged off the disturbance with a toss of her head, and carried on her way with her tail gently wagging.

The smells of the street made Tess want to investigate the fish-and-chip shop, the greengrocer's, and entrances to the pubs. It was near to closing time and so she came into contact with a lot of emerging feet. This contact with new people and different environments was a most necessary part of Tess's early experience. She was also "busy" a couple of times in the gutter, quite unalarmed by the fact that cars were passing just a couple of yards from her.

49

In front of the bakery on the other side of the street, Edith recognised another puppy-walker and her charge, a seven-month-old labrador bitch called Quaker. Edith thought it would be good for Tess to meet the older animal and they crossed over to the other side. The smells from the bakery set Tess's nostrils twitching, but it was Quaker which interested her most. Although Quaker was on her lead, she moved at once to inspect the puppy, nearly pulling her handler over in the process—proof that the way ahead for Edith and Tess would not necessarily be plain sailing! Quaker was corrected and made to sit, and she patiently waited for Tess to finish sniffing at her. Then the animals rubbed noses, and calmed down. Tess was now a little tired and not as boisterous as she might have been earlier.

It was a very tired puppy which eventually returned to number 59, and after going out into the garden for a moment Tess climbed into her bed and was instantly asleep.

Over the next three weeks, Tess got through a lot of basic training. She became better about leaving the house on her leash, although there was still some reluctance. She was wormed again and was clear; she was eating well and causing no concern. She had shown a wish to dig in the garden, and Ken was resigned to the fact that this was going to be yet another year with no

Puppy-walkers and supervisor happen to meet and for a moment there is chaos as the dogs meet too.

flowers at the back of the house. Zoë had been simply dreadful in the garden—as Ken put in the bedding-plants, the puppy carefully dug them up again and placed them at his feet, and no amount of cajoling could persuade her to leave them. He even tried putting in the plants at night, but as soon as Zoë was free she dug them up again.

Tess was taken to the centre of Southam several times, and her confidence grew with every visit. She wasn't always on her best behaviour, and on more than one occasion she would have been off like a shot after a rapidly disappearing cat had Edith not kept a firm grip on the lead. Most dogs will chase cats if the cats run, and although Tess had been introduced to the resident tabbies at Tollgate House, those animals are so used to dogs that they never run away from them. Countless dogs are killed on the roads each year through mindlessly pursuing running cats, so it is important for all dog-owners to train their animals not to react to their movements—and in the case of guide dogs that training has to be 100% successful.

Tess also disgraced herself at the florist's by knocking over a display. Not much was broken, though some of the plants took a battering. The owners were used to mishaps like that, and refused all of Edith's offers to pay for the damage. Edith took the opportunity of walking Tess back and forth past the bright display, correcting any move she made towards it.

Order is restored.

Ken reassures Tess while allowing her to get used to noisy road works.

They went into all the shops in the town—the baker's, the butcher's, the newsagent's and the greengrocer's—meeting new people every day. The shopkeepers made a great fuss of Tess, and those who didn't know better offered her tit-bits. Edith had to refuse them all because a guide dog has to learn to eat only at mealtimes and never to accept "treats". There were one or two near things though, like the time Tess accidentally knocked a packet of crisps from a display and was close to eating them before Edith could get them away from her.

By the time Tess was ten weeks old, she was completely house-trained. She had rarely been left on her own for long during the day, and hadn't shown any of the characteristic signs of boredom—like destroying anything chewable—and so it was a cheerful Edith who greeted Alison on the supervisor's first visit.

Alison checked with Edith on the puppy's behaviour and feeding; she was pleased to hear that there were no problems with house-training, and interested in the animal's reluctance to leave the house on her lead. Then

52

Alison took Tess out, following the same route Edith had taken on their first walk. The puppy was still difficult to get started, but the experienced supervisor was very firm with her and Tess responded, although she obviously wanted to stay where she was. She pulled out in front quite a lot, but reacted well to increased tension on the lead, and as long as Alison kept correcting her, Tess walked quite well. It is most important that guide dog puppies learn the correct way to walk, because unlike most dogs, which are trained to walk to heel, the guide dog will have to lead the way.

They met some other dogs, and Tess's friendly but cautious greetings showed Alison that she had been well schooled. Although compared with a fully grown pup Tess was still very green, the signs were that she was going in the right direction.

Then Alison popped Tess into her car and drove into the centre of Southam. She wanted to look for signs of the sensitivity which had worried Derek Freeman when Tess was very young, but the puppy had now experienced Southam at its busiest, and there was nothing there to frighten her. This was just what Alison had hoped to see, and after a ten-minute stroll round the shops she took the puppy home.

"I think she's ready for a walk in a really busy place now," Alison told Edith on their return. "But make sure she has all her innoculations before she's fourteen weeks old, and let us have the bill."

Then she was off on her next visit, promising to be back in a month.
The very next morning, Edith and Tess went on the bus into Leamington with Ken. There was a moment's amusement as the little puppy struggled to get onto the bus before getting a helping hand under the rump from Edith. Guide dogs are trained to travel under the seat on public transport wherever possible so as not to interfere with their blind owners or other passengers. Most dogs learn this quite quickly, but on this first trip Tess tried to get out several times, tangling her lead with the nearest pair of legs, and once she tried to climb onto the lap of a lady in the seat behind. But mostly she lay quiet where she was put.

Leamington Spa is a lovely town, with wide streets and plenty of greenery and parks. They left the bus, and Ken went on to the bank while Edith and Tess walked down the road past the Pump Room. There was a lot of early morning traffic, and although Tess certainly registered the noise and smell, she didn't shy away.

The town walk was a great success. The little puppy experienced all sorts of new things; the noisiest was a pneumatic drill and road-leveller, and the most confusing was a set of revolving doors. Tess approached the roadworks without fear, even though her ears twitched at the noise, and Edith knew that

Ken introduces Tess to a difficult open staircase.

her sensitive streak had all but vanished. Just past the Town Hall is an old-fashioned hotel with revolving doors, and Edith decided to let Tess try them. The staff in the foyer glanced up as they entered—Tess on Edith's left in the widest part of the revolve—and then immediately continued out into the street; the hotel staff were used to this as trainers from the Leamington centre as well as puppy-walkers regularly bring their charges there. Edith and Tess negotiated the door four times, and when they went back into the street the puppy received well-earned and necessary praise: Tess was obviously very intelligent and a quick learner.

After about half an hour, Edith called in at the bank to say goodbye to Ken, before going down the road to a milk bar for a cup of coffee. Tess was made to sit under the table, and Edith had to refuse the occasional piece of chocolate or biscuit that was offered to the animal as she rested; she knew that it wouldn't take Tess long to refuse the tit-bits on her own account.

Before going to catch their bus they visited the park. Once they were well away from the traffic, Edith let Tess off her leash and, keeping between the

54

Edith always uses zebra crossings if possible so that Tess will learn to recognise them.

animal and the route to the road, let her have a run. They moved into the centre of the park towards the bridge over the river. There were one or two geese and swans on the water and a lot of ducks. To avoid any mishaps with either the water or the birds, Edith re-fastened the puppy's lead, and they then strolled along the river bank.

Neither of them saw the mute swan until it was almost too late. It rose sharply from the edge of the water behind a bush and suddenly it was barring their path, its wings spreading in a threatening gesture. Tess looked surprised as the swan hissed at her, and Edith gave a sharp tug on the leash to get her to retrace her steps. The puppy responded to the tension at once but as they took a detour Tess kept her eyes firmly fixed on the new creature. The swan stood still for a moment, holding its long neck aloof, before giving a final warning flap of its wings and settling down again behind the bush.

Tess was beginning to show signs of tiring, and Edith led her over the iron-sided bridge and up the slope at the far side which would bring them to the bus station. On the way back to Southam, the puppy was so tired that she slept under the seat for the whole journey.

A week later, after Tess had had her innoculations, Edith took her to Leamington again. The puppy was now responding well to control in the street. The roadworks had moved some way up the hill, and Tess observed the noisy machinery without any apprehension. But she was very alert, and seemed intrigued by the fact that a workman's head kept appearing and disappearing into a hole, and Edith had to restrain her from going over for a closer investigation.

Edith had to persuade her to enter the revolving doors again, but once she was in them she was raring to go and had to be steadied down—puppies can be very boisterous, and far from being sensitive, there were times when Tess was being too bold. This would need careful handling, because being too bold is almost as bad a fault as being too timid, and the aim is for the puppies to be steady in everything.

Ken was able to take a little time off work to join them and as Tess had now mastered the staircase at home he took her on the open stairway behind the Town Hall. This was an interesting experience for Tess. She stopped once or twice because she could see through the metalwork, and had to be persuaded to continue, but after her initial wariness she tackled the obstacle bravely. They went up and down several times and by the end of the exercise Tess knew there was nothing to fear from the open gaps. Everything she might come into contact with in the future had to be experienced at the earliest possible time.

As they walked on through the town, Edith was meticulous in always crossing the road at zebra crossings—it was important for Tess to recognise the markings as indicating the correct place to cross—and in waiting for vehicles to come to a halt at traffic lights. This helped to prepare Tess for the time when she would have to decide whether it was safe for her blind owner to leave the pavement.

Later, Edith sat down on a bench overlooking the river, with Tess at her feet. Every time Tess sat, Edith would correct her position. Labradors are often sloppy sitters, and tend to splay out their back legs, which makes them look lopsided. The correct position is for them to be as compact as possible, and that was especially important for an animal whose owner would be blind—a protruding leg could be a hazard.

Edith then carried out another basic training move. With Tess sitting, she held the leash in her right hand, close to the pup's collar under the chin, put her left hand on the animal's shoulders, and then, pulling down with her right and pushing down with her left hand, firmly and calmly said "down". The puppy couldn't resist and went flat, and Edith praised her. She didn't stay down for more than a second or two, and Edith repeated the exercise three or four times until Tess appeared to "get the message". Edith always tried to contain her training to short intensive lessons, so that the puppy wouldn't have time to get bored, and always to end a session on a success. And Tess did her proud.

On their way back to get the bus, they met a trainer from the local centre, together with a bitch on her advanced training. Tess wanted to play, but on a word from the trainer his animal just sat down, and although she watched Tess with great interest and her tail swept back and forth on the ground, her body stayed in the sitting position. Tess didn't learn by example!

"She's a bright little thing, isn't she?" said the trainer.

"I think she's the nicest one I've had," said Edith.

"Better than Zoë?" he asked.

"Well, I was just learning myself, then," said Edith with a laugh. "I don't think that Tess is going to be quite such hard work."

"Still, it's early days yet. She might become a real terror."

And they both laughed before setting off in opposite directions.

When Alison called on her second visit, Matthew and Lisa were at home for their half-term holiday, and the supervisor was interested to hear how the children got on with the puppy.

"She's ever so good," answered Lisa. "I made her sit and stay in the field, and she didn't come until I called her. She's really clever."

"Can we come, too?" asked Matthew, as Alison prepared to take Tess out.

57

"I'd rather you didn't," said Alison. "It just might distract her, and I have to see for myself how well she's progressing."

For the Washingtons it was just like waiting for an exam result, but when Alison returned, she was full of praise for the way that they had been training Tess.

The report Alison made back at Tollgate House showed that Tess's sensitivity appeared to have gone, that the puppy's innoculations were complete, and she was progressing well. She was quiet on her leash, and friendly, and the children were doing a lot to help. She told Derek that Lisa had said she wanted to work with dogs when she left school.

"That's it. Catch 'em young," thought Derek.

Tess's daily walks in Southam and Leamington continued, and Edith took her into all the busiest areas. The puppy seemed happy in any environment—high street, park, bank, garage forecourts, narrow alleys, open boulevards. As far as Tess was concerned, everywhere was "out" and that meant fun and exercise. Edith tried to end each walk with a game in the park and, if they had been to Leamington, that meant that on the way home Tess would lie still under the seat in the bus. At just about four months old, she was now taking up this position instinctively, and it was a habit she would never lose.

Then, four days before Alison was due to make her third visit, Tess disappeared.

Edith had put her into the garden before taking her out for her morning walk, while she finished tidying the house. A quarter of an hour later when she went to call the puppy, Tess was not in the garden.

Edith called Tess loudly, but there was no response. She went to the end of the garden and looked out into the grass alley outside, but she knew that there was no way Tess could have got out that way. As she turned back towards the house, she saw to her horror that the wrought-iron gate to the side passage of the house was open. That was where Matthew kept his bike, and Edith recalled that Matthew had taken his bike to school that day to practise for a school slow-bicycle race; he must have left the gate open.

By now Edith was too worried to feel angry at the boy's carelessness. She ran through the gate into the front garden, which was open to the pavement and the street. She called the puppy again, hoping against hope that she would see the little yellow bitch come bounding back to her, all head, tail and legs waggling. But there was no sign of her.

Edith thought Tess would most likely have headed for the playground, so she rushed that way. She passed some neighbours, but they hadn't seen the

59

Awaiting the order
to get off the bus.

puppy, nor had the mums at the swings. Without pausing, Edith ran across the field, calling Tess's name. Her spirits began to fall as she came to the road, and her relief at not seeing the pup dead in the road was tempered with growing anxiety because she had not found Tess on their normal route.

Then she was outside the school, where the children were having their mid-morning break. Edith's heart lifted as she saw a group of boys in a huddle around something, and Matthew was among them. "They've got her," she thought, her heart pounding with relief and from the exertion of her sprint around the field. But her hopes were shattered as a teacher moved up to the group to break up the fight the boys had been watching.

The teacher was reprimanding the two culprits as Edith hurried up. "I'm sorry to come barging in, but I've lost our puppy," Edith blurted out, and went straight on, "Matthew, you left the gate open and she's gone."

"I didn't, Mum, honest," said the boy.

"You must have—you came with your bike this morning, didn't you?"

Before she could continue, the teacher told Matthew to get his bike and help his mother look for the puppy, and promised to ask all the children to keep a look-out for her.

Edith calmed down, thanked the teacher, and hastened out of the school playground. Matthew soon caught her up on his bike, and she told him to ride around looking, and ask anyone he saw if they had seen the puppy. He rode off calling Tess's name. Edith took a deep breath and tried to think of the things she was supposed to do in these circumstances. It had all been in the handbook she had been given when she became a puppy-walker. She knew she should check the main shops, call at the vet's, and report the matter to the police. When she left the house she had deliberately left the gate and the back door open so that should Tess make her own way home, she could get in.

It was a miserable Edith who after an hour and a half's search completed her tour of the town. At the police station, the desk sergeant had been very helpful and had promised that his men would keep a look-out for the stray, but Edith had wanted to weep. Maybe Tess was trapped somewhere; worse, maybe she was dead. Walking sadly back to the house, Edith occasionally called the puppy's name, but now with very little hope of finding her. When Matthew cycled up, his expression showed that he too had been unsuccessful—he had been everywhere, he said, even to the senior school, but no one had seen Tess.

Matthew parked his bike in the side passage. He was full of remorse. It was all his fault, he thought, as he closed the heavy gate he had neglected to shut in the morning.

"I'll run away," he said to himself irrationally as he crept up the stairs.

Edith decided to phone Ken and had just started to dial the number when she heard a shout from above.

"Tess! Tess, you're all right. Mum! Mum! Tess is here, Mum. She's all right. Oh you lovely dog."

Edith left the phone dangling, took the stairs two at a time, and burst into Matthew's room.

Tess really liked continental quilts, and the newly awakened puppy was still partly underneath the quilt on Matthew's bed. She was very surprised to be the subject of so much attention and praise, as she had just woken up and so far as she knew, hadn't done anything to merit it. In fact she wasn't aware that she had done anything at all. Edith hugged and patted the puppy, delighted that she was well and in her safekeeping once more. Of course Tess should not have been in Matthew's bed, but this was no time for a training lesson.

That evening, the Washingtons were able to laugh over the alarm; they would never know whether Tess had been "walkabout" or whether she had been under the quilt all the time.

"At least I shall check all the rooms in the house before I get into such a panic again," Edith told Alison when the supervisor came for her third visit.

Once again, Alison took Tess out on her own, gave her some "free running" in the field and tested her on re-call. Then she put her in the back of the Mini Clubman with two other pups she was testing, and drove into Leamington Spa. The dogs were free in the cage at the back of the car, and this gave Alison an opportunity to observe whether they travelled well, and how they related to each other in the close confines of a moving vehicle.

They all behaved very well in the town. Tess was still very interested in passers-by and was easily distracted—concentration would come much later. She responded to the occasional controlling jerk on her leash, and she was leading out quite well, but she had a tendency to pull away to the left and Alison had little success in making her keep on a straighter line.

The supervisor could see that Tess was progressing well, and that Edith was doing her job admirably. The puppy had been exposed to new experiences according to schedule; she was eating three meals a day, and her discipline was improving, though she needed a lot of practice in re-call when she was playing in the field. Alison warned Edith to expect Tess to begin teething soon and to make sure she got some marrow bones from the butcher so that Tess could gnaw on them rather than anything else in the house. There had been an unfortunate case of a teething puppy eating a family's budgie!

Tess got through her teething with very little trouble, but while it lasted her obedience deteriorated and she was inclined to be naughty. But this was only a phase which seemed very much on the mend by the time she was 22 weeks old and Alison made her fourth visit.

This time Edith took the dog out, and Alison was the observer and occasional distraction. Tess coped admirably, and Edith was quite proud as the puppy led out along the streets and shopping area with which she had become so familiar. There were moments when she pulled too much on her lead, and she seemed to be developing a sort of "crabbing" walk which Alison had to show Edith how to correct. It was something on which they would have to concentrate when they were out on their own, she said. One really good point was that Tess was responding very much more to vocal commands than to restraint from the lead, which was an important stage in her development.

When the bitches come into season, some puppy-walkers look after them at home, but Edith preferred to send them back to Tollgate House for the full 21 days. This would give Tess the experience of living in kennels again, as she would do for her later training, and Derek Freeman and his assistants could assess her progress and see how she behaved.

So Tess came back to the place where she was born, and went into a kennel with two puppies of approximately the same age. There were eighteen bitches in residence at the centre at the time, including two brood bitches about to whelp and three others which had been brought to the centre for mating.

Tess took a little time to settle into kennels, but after a couple of days she seemed very much at home and was eating well and enjoying her daily exercise in the fenced open runs.

"I thought she would probably be smallish," Derek said to Alison over lunch one day in the staff dining room at Tollgate House, "but she's quite a good size."

"I think she's about average in every way," Alison replied. "I'm sure she'll do very well. She doesn't like change much, and that makes her a wee bit sensitive, but she soon got used to the kennels, and I've never had any bother with her on her walks."

After three weeks without training, Edith found Tess a little bit rusty when she came back to Southam, but the puppy hadn't forgotten her voice, and her responses were soon back to normal. Soon, she began to show much more prolonged concentration.

Tess was now rising eight months old, and her obedience was quite good. She was quiet on her lead, and the distractions which disturbed her concentration were getting fewer and fewer all the time. She would mostly "leave" things when told; her re-call on the word "come" was improving; but she still had a lot of difficulty with "stay": she would always edge forward in a sly attempt to follow, though as long as she was watched she would stay put.

One day Edith took Tess on the train from Leamington to Coventry. The puppy showed no concern as the diesel approached the platform, and needed no encouragement to lead on through the open carriage door. She sat peacefully under the seat, undisturbed by the noise and movement on the train.

The trip gave Edith an opportunity of walking Tess in a town with which neither of them was familiar: one got so used to certain routes that variety was essential. They walked through the pedestrian area in the centre of the city, passed by the Cathedral, rode in a lift in the car park, wandered among the crowds in the shops, crossed busy roads, and sat for a while watching the buses at the terminus before going back to the station to catch the train to Leamington.

As it was now five-thirty, they met Ken at the bank and went to have a drink in a pub before catching the bus. Tess had rested in the train and was very alert and boisterous, but she was calmed by Edith's command and settled at her feet.

A kindly old man offered Tess a biscuit. Edith was about to ask him not to when she realised that Tess wasn't going to take it anyway.

"Go on, girl, aren't you hungry?" the man asked.

"She's a guide dog," said Edith proudly.

"Don't they get hungry then?" the man replied with a twinkle in his eye. And they all laughed.

On the way home, Ken asked Edith about their next dog. He wondered if they could have a black labrador this time, as he was fed up with brushing light hairs off his suits. Edith had already asked Alison about this, and had been told that there would be no problem if they were prepared to wait. Ken was obviously pleased, but told Edith that if it would take long he wouldn't mind another yellow one. "What's a few dog hairs anyway," he added.

The annual Breeders and Puppy-walkers' Day is held at Tollgate House each June. Most people walking dogs on the scheme try to be there for the event, which gives all the Association's helpers, both experienced and inexperienced, an opportunity to learn more about how guide dogs are trained. There is a series of competitions, and the staff can see how the trainee puppies react to the presence of so many others. Once again the weather was just right, and the sun shone brightly as perhaps two thousand people and about

63

three hundred dogs wandered round the grounds. The large lawn in front of the house was marked out as a show arena.

Edith and Ken had a chat with Derek Freeman, who told them that he had decided that from "T" litter he was going to keep Tara back for brood, and that Tess would go on her advanced training in about six weeks. A call from the house sent him scurrying away, and the Washingtons went back to the front lawn for the opening speech.

Then the competitions began in the show ring. There were prizes for the best condition puppy under six months old, the best over six months old, the best child handler (Lisa and Tess came fourth), the best condition brood bitch and stud dog, and there was even a fancy dress parade. It was, as always, a most enjoyable day out for both those taking part and the spectators; there were things to laugh at and things to learn, and above all there was a feeling that everyone there knew they were helping to do something really worthwhile.

The Annual Breeders and Puppy-walkers' Day at Tollgate House—this puppy just can't wait to go.

The fancy dress parade is put on specially for the children, but it does look as if they're not the only ones to enjoy it.

Derek Freeman breeds his shepherd dogs so carefully that his seven-year-old twins can take almost any liberty with them.

Just as the Washingtons were about to leave, Derek came over and told Edith that he thought there would be a black lab puppy for her about six weeks after Tess was returned. That helped to make Edith's day, though her pleasure was tempered with the knowledge that Tess, like Zoë and Melody, would soon be leaving her to continue her training, and that she would not see her again. After rearing a puppy for the first ten months of its life it was hard not to be sad when the time came for parting.

The next six weeks passed very quickly, too quickly for Edith. Tess had been a delight to train; she had learned quickly, and avoided most of the mishaps which could have befallen her. Puppies often have to have treatment for cuts and abrasions, and sometimes even for broken limbs. Tess had been lucky, and she was a healthy normal puppy of slightly higher than average intelligence, with a lovely nature.

Edith would miss her dreadfully—until she got involved with her next charge.

Part Three
Wokingham

CHAPTER ONE: Re-assessment and Early Training

FROM THE DAY Alison collected her from the Washingtons' home and drove her back to Tollgate House, Tess's puppy days were over. She was now regarded by the Association as an adult bitch, and would be housed in kennels until her training was completed and she was handed over to her blind owner. But that was still a long way in the future, and for the next sixteen days Barrie Stocks would take over.

As Derek Freeman's assistant, Barrie had been responsible for the original mating of Harmony and Tango which had produced "T" litter. Now, a year later, he had to assess the young adult dogs' potential before allocating them to one of the Association's training centres at Exeter, Bolton, Leamington, Forfar and Wokingham. Every month, as the puppy-walkers return their charges for reassessment, the breeding centre sends out lists to the training centres, telling them how many animals of which breed would be available for advanced training at the end of the month.

When Tess was returned to Tollgate House, the other new arrivals were nine labradors, five gold retrievers, five german shepherds (alsatians), and four crossbreeds. It took all the animals a little time to settle into their new surroundings, and Tess took a little longer than most. She obviously didn't like change much, and perhaps she was pining for Edith as well.

Barrie's job in reassessing the young dogs was thorough and painstaking, but not without its lighter side. One of the curly-coats had come back to Tollgate House as a potential stud dog but there was a black mark on his record card—there was a note which suggested that he was dreadful with cats. Barrie decided to test whether this fault was serious by putting one of the centre's resident cats into the run with a labrador bitch which was just coming into season. Then he introduced the dog to the run, and not surprisingly the cat was ignored!

One of the labrador bitches didn't seem to like the stairs inside the main building, though she was quite happy with stairs and steps outside. Barrie found out from Marion Broughall, the dog's walking supervisor, that the animal had been living in a bungalow. There was an easy cure for that fault. Marion, whom the bitch knew and liked, went to the top of the stairs and as she called the labrador's name, Barrie made a loud noise from behind the animal. The surprised dog found that she was at the top of the stairs before she had time to realise what she was doing, and she was greeted by the customary praise for something done well. After the exercise had been repeated a few times the problem was as good as over.

The dogs were exercised in the grass runs every day, and Barrie took four or five of them into Leamington for a town walk. The fact that he was not known to the animals was offset by his experience and authority when dealing with them. It was a time for meticulous observation. There must be no mistake now, for although the animals had not so far been a great drain on the Association's resources, they were going to cost a lot of money from now on. Any animal which failed to make the grade would have to be rejected, and this was the fate of one of the german shepherds, whose suspected hip-displacement was confirmed under x-ray. This disability is not an uncommon reason for rejecting potential guide dogs, but it is not something which prevents a dog from being a wonderful pet, so the Association's loss would be a private owner's gain.

None of the animals in the reassessment group was perfect—Tess still "crabbed" a little as she walked, one or two others sat very badly, and some failed to respond very well to Barrie's voice, but from now on they were going to be in the hands of professional instructors, and would improve rapidly.

Most of the dogs in the group were to go to the Leamington centre, but three were going to Bolton, five to Exeter and Tess, with a german shepherd bitch, was off to the training centre at Wokingham. They were to fill the "topping up" requirement there. Barrie Stocks arranged to meet Brian Moody, the controller at Wokingham, half-way between the two centres for the changeover. Barrie always tried to deliver the animals himself so that he could be in touch with the trainers. So just after noon one day Barrie's estate car pulled into the service area on the Oxford–Banbury road. Brian Moody and his assistant Lesley Malcolm were already waiting in the café.

"What have you got for us then, Barrie?" asked Brian, as they collected their coffee.

"The alsatian, Sheba. You'll have no trouble with her—she's very steady and not too big. The lab's called Tess, and she's lovely. We thought at first that she was a bit on the sensitive side, but she isn't really. She doesn't seem to like her handler changing, but she soon gets over that."

They chatted about the dogs for a few moments before going back to the car park, where the two bitches were unloaded from Barrie's car. Brian and Lesley made a great fuss of them both. As she was led away Tess looked over her shoulder at Barrie, but this was no time for sentiment. The essence of a good guide dog is its adaptability; a real bond must be formed between

68

No disorderly conduct allowed!

handler and dog, but when the handler changes the dog must adapt quickly to the new one, and ultimately to its blind owner.

Both dogs travelled well on the journey to Wokingham, and the dark estate car eventually turned into the drive of Folly Court, one of the training centres of the Guide Dogs for the Blind Association. It was opened on 12 May 1977 by HRH Princess Alexandra, and has since become the Association's showpiece. Apart from the main block, which retains some features of the original mansion, the whole complex was purpose built, from the blind students' bedrooms and social areas to the three kennel blocks behind the main buildings. A red notice beside the tree-lined drive warns drivers "Blind People and Dogs in Training".

Lesley Malcolm took the two dogs from the back of the car and led them round the pathway to the intake block, which would be their home during the next three weeks while they were being assessed by the early training unit. As they reached the lower end of the complex they came into sight of the main kennels, and Sheba and Tess showed a lot of interest in the residents, who came bounding up to the fences, barking out greetings. The noise was alarming, but the two newcomers had already learned that the lead meant "work", and neither tried to join in the general shindig.

Dogs out in the run during Early Training. Even during these free running periods Lesley reinforces discipline by making them all "sit and stay".

The early training Tess was about to commence would not seem very different to her from all she had done before as a pup, but the standard she would be required to achieve would be very much higher. All the trainers know that the perfect animal does not exist, but though all the dogs on the training course would make lots of mistakes, these would be worked on over and over again to ensure that the animals were safe when they were finally handed over as qualified guide dogs. It would take six months of gruelling work, but at the end of it all, one more blind person would have the opportunity to be mobile and independent. That was the ultimate aim for each new arrival at the Wokingham Training Centre.

Each monthly intake is put under the charge of an instructor and up to five training assistants. After three months in the early training unit, the dogs are handed over to different instructors for advanced training. That too lasts three months, and is followed by a one-month course with the future guide

First lesson in retrieving.

dog owners. All these courses run concurrently, so the Wokingham centre is a constant hive of activity. Brian Moody is the controller of all the work of the centre, and he keeps in touch with every instructor, blind student and dog in the establishment. It is a great tribute to him and his staff that the building functions so efficiently. Mike Csernovits, the head instructor, supervises the dogs and trainers, and there is a kennel manager in charge of the animals' welfare. The supporting staff includes a resident matron, a housekeeper and an administrator, together with their assistants, and the centre operates like a very efficient factory, but with the personal touches that make it a genuinely friendly community.

Not the least important member of the staff at each training centre is the resident guide dog owner. At Wokingham, Lorna acts as general receptionist and secretary, but she is also important in helping the students, as the future guide dog owners are called. Many of them will never have had the opportunity of mixing with so many blind people before they come to the centre for the one-month residential training course, and Lorna not only helps them feel at ease but can discuss any problems they have handling their dogs with an understanding born of experience.

It's extremely useful to the blind owner if the dog has been taught to retrieve as lots of exercise can then be given even with limited space and time.

But it would be six months before Tess would meet her future owner, and she was just about to begin her first walk with her new trainer. She had been allocated to Lesley Malcolm, along with another labrador bitch, Bonnie, and a german shepherd called Lenny. Lesley observed them carefully on the first walk. The time had been carefully chosen—the council dustmen were collecting rubbish from the bins, providing plenty of distraction. Lenny, the alsatian, walked very well and wasn't the least perturbed by the lumbering refuse truck, but he caught sight of a flock of pigeons on the grass and barked furiously at them, and it took a very firm hand to keep him under control until they had flown off. This was going to be quite a problem for his trainer, and if his discipline did not improve he would have to be rejected.

Bonnie's problem on this first walk was that every time they met another dog she instantly tried to get to it, and she strained towards the open runs from where the inmates barked at her. But Lesley stayed in control, and thought this problem could be overcome.

Tess walked well, although her rear end did stick out a little, and she caused the least trouble of the three. As they approached the dustbin area, one of the metal containers was just being lowered from the truck, reaching

73

Lesley taking Tess round "off-kerb" obstacles in the grounds of Folly Court.

the ground with a resounding clatter. Tess looked nervous for just a second, turning her head sharply to identify where the noise came from, and she set off a little faster than before. However, without any correction she soon slowed down to normal walking pace.

Over the next week, all the dogs in the early training unit were taken out twice a day. They were expected to respond to firm voice control, and they began to be taught to look for the straightest line to walk, and not to cut corners. They were corrected if they showed any desire to scavenge from the paths or gutters. They walked in different parts of Wokingham, and in between times they went into the long grassy runs at the centre for play and for practising general obedience. This was kept down to about ten minutes each day—long enough for the dogs to learn, but not so long that they got bored.

In the second week the dogs were made to sit in the correct position at every kerb they came to. This was going to be an important part of their future work, for they would have to sit until their owners decided that a road was safe to cross. They also had to learn the difference between an "up" kerb and a "down" kerb—it would be dangerous if after successfully negotiating a busy street an animal was to sit before mounting the pavement!

Tess was taken to the new shopping precinct in Bracknell, which had areas with railings through which she could look down on shoppers in the square below; there were also subways and escalators, and they visited the bus and railway stations. Although the dogs had already experienced places like these, training was now in earnest, and no puppyish behaviour could be indulged. This meant a lot of voice control by the trainers and Tess, like the other dogs, had to be "talked through" difficult situations to maintain her concentration. They experienced crowds, lifts, pavements, shops and road junctions over and over again, and each time a higher standard of response was expected from them.

At the beginning of the fourth week Tess was introduced to the bodypiece of her harness. Some dogs baulk at this at first, but like most of her group Tess accepted it calmly. After a few days the handle was attached: the handles are about 18 inches long and fall easily to hand beside the body when the dog is leading on correctly. From then on, the dogs would always work in full harness with an additional check lead, exactly as they would work with their blind owners.

Tess also had to learn to negotiate obstacles, including those which she, but not a grown man or woman, could walk underneath. She learned to ignore distractions, and artificial distractions were used to reinforce her concentration, such as another trainer calling her name, or a boisterous animal being

75

At one of the first "sit and stay" lessons Tess is under the impression that Lesley is going to play with her, but under Lesley's patient tuition she soon learns to "sit" as Lesley backs away from her.

brought up to her when she was working. It is extraordinary how the dogs learn these lessons; in harness they gradually become steadier, but remain playful and friendly when out of it.

When she was a week short of thirteen months old, Tess came into her second season, and the intensity of her training was reduced for a couple of weeks. It is normal procedure for prospective guide dog bitches to be spayed: a bitch in season can be a problem for any owner, let alone one who cannot see. So at fourteen and a half months Tess had her operation. She took it very well, and recuperated for a fortnight in the hospital kennels. Her training was a little bit rusty for a few days afterwards, but she soon got back into the routine, and within a week she was back in training and seemed to have a more adult approach to her work.

The training assistants now reinforced the command of "forward" with "straight on" each time they moved off, and Tess was already beginning to look for the straight line herself. She was now being given fifteen minutes of

Feed-time: the dogs are not allowed to jump around, but have to sit down in an orderly manner. Even when their bowls are put on the ground they must not touch the food until the go-ahead.

concentrated obedience training each day, practising "sits", "downs" and "stays", and also her re-call. Tess was good at that, always bounding happily back to her trainer as soon as she was called. Again, an essential lesson—a blind person cannot go chasing after an animal which does not respond to that instruction.

There were new skills to learn, too, such as a left turn. Imagine the situation when a dog is sitting at the kerb, facing the road, with its blind owner on its right. If the dog stood and turned left, it could well jettison the handler over the kerb and into the road, or into the nearest lamp-post. So the dog learns to turn right about, bringing them both into the centre of the pavement and away from danger. Simple, but very important, and Tess learnt that too. She understood new words of command—if she walked too close to her handler, "over" meant that she had to move away, and "in" meant closer. Again and again Tess's trainer repeated the lessons until the response from the labrador was good. Then they would be repeated until it became excellent! The same commands helped her negotiate obstacles and ensure that she would always

78

leave enough room for her handler to avoid them too.

By the end of her three months early training, Tess had become a good steady animal. Her "crabbing" had all but disappeared, and she was looking a very good prospect indeed. She had spent several nights on her dog-bed in the corner of her trainer's room so that her domestic behaviour could be assessed, and had shown that she would be good in a home environment. She had already achieved a standard of obedience that most dog-owners would envy, and she still had three months of advanced training to go.

Tess is washed and given a luxurious blow dry.

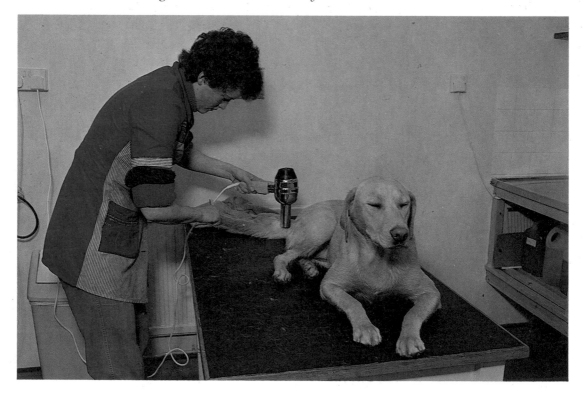

CHAPTER TWO: Advanced Training

THERE WERE fifteen dogs in Tess's advanced group. The senior instructor, Dave Griffiths, and his colleagues had observed the dogs during their early training, and over the first few days the instructors on the advanced course aimed to maintain their charges' previous training and wait until they got to know each other before trying anything new. Tess was one of five animals which would be trained by the assistant instructor, Becky Oldfield. They soon built up a good relationship, and Tess took less time than before to adapt to her new handler. The dogs now practised obedience for fifteen minutes a day, and their responses became even sharper.

By the beginning of her third week of advanced training, Tess was as proficient as any dog on the course. She was walked on the pavement along the busy Oxford road, but showed no fear or alarm. No dog can be taught that traffic is dangerous, but a guide dog must know that a moving vehicle means "stop". Tess was now taught to disobey incorrect instructions. Even during early training, she had been instructed "forward" when a car was approaching. Her first instinct had been to obey, but she had been stopped, and the moving vehicle pointed out to her. The reinforcement of that disobedience was one of the most important aspects of her advanced training.

Traffic of course comes from both directions, and the dogs have to be taught to be aware of both "near" and "far" traffic. At the centre, artificial situations were created where the dogs had to stop and sit in the middle of the road when "far" traffic came up fast and unexpectedly. As the training progressed, the dogs were placed in increasingly perilous and complicated situations, situations which would be commonplace after they had qualified but which they should if possible encounter for the first time while they were in the hands of qualified instructors.

The dogs had to become "safe", and although they all made mistakes, the instructors would patiently correct them and try again. Tess proved to be better than average, and after four weeks was having a pretty good success rate. It was intense work. There were three training sessions every two days, and the dogs were now required to take very much more of the responsibility when out on a walk—it had been less than 20% at the end of her early training, but now 75% was needed.

Becky often practised re-call with Tess in an enclosed space at the centre, and she was expected, even when running free, to ignore outside distractions. Every action had to be second nature to her. Her turns were reinforced. She went into both town and country areas. She learned to be unafraid of high-speed trains passing in front of her at Reading Station, and how to lead the way on to all forms of public transport. When a lesson was apparently learned, her instructor would deliberately try to catch her out—all part of reinforcing her concentration. Some people may think that the guide dog is always in control, but at a road crossing the dog must wait for the "forward" command from its handler. Then the dog takes over and decides whether or not to obey, and is able to correct any mistake its blind owner may make. Traffic situations are artificially created in the grounds of Folly Court to give extra tuition to any animal which needs it, but Tess seemed to be doing well and this was not necessary for her.

Her training walks generally lasted for about 20 minutes. She visited shops and cafés, where she demonstrated how well she had been schooled by Edith. Then at the end of the sixth week, the instructors took all fifteen dogs up to London.

The Association's van was parked in the underground car park at Hyde Park, and one at a time the animals were taken out on a walk. After a few moments free-running in the park, Tess responded well to her re-call, in spite of the hum of the traffic in Park Lane, and the numerous distractions like people, pigeons and litter. On the way up Park Lane to Speaker's Corner, Tess delicately avoided four Arab gentlemen in their flowing robes who spread across the pavement in front of her, steering a wide enough course for her instructor not to get bumped. In fact Tess had been given a lot of "right-shoulder training" because she had a tendency to cut it a bit fine when avoiding obstacles, but she was now pretty well cured.

They crossed beneath Marble Arch by the subway, and Tess was very alert. She cocked her ears to identify the sound of some buskers singing to a guitar, but after seeing them she made no attempt to go up to them, and continued in as straight a line as the other pedestrians would allow. Up the stairs they went, and then down into the bowels of the London Underground. With occasional promptings, Tess led the way through the maze of passages. As they approached the platform, a rush of passengers poured out of one of the tunnels, but in spite of the newness, noisiness and bustle, Tess stayed quite calm.

On the eastbound platform, Tess and Becky walked a little way along, the dog keeping to the centre so that her companion was well away from the platform edge. When Becky stopped, Tess sat facing the rails, about four feet from the edge. After a few seconds there was the echoing rumble of a train approaching, its arrival signalled by a rush of warm air. Tess turned her head

Becky training Tess in traffic—in particular to sit automatically if a car approaches when they are half way across the road, even if she has been told to go "forward". This is called "trained dis-obedience" and is one of the most advanced things that Tess will have to learn.

Even at this advanced stage much of the training is still in the grounds of Folly Court. Here Becky is taking Tess (or being taken, perhaps) through the obstacle course. Tess has to learn to go round overhead obstacles up to 6 ft high which she could easily go under, but which would result in a nasty bump for her blind owner.

into the strengthening breeze: she had often seen trains, but this was the first time she had come into contact with one in an enclosed space. It caused her no problems. The long silver snake of the Central Line train burst into view at the left end of the platform, and the breeze dropped as it glided to a stop. The carriage doors opened with a loud hiss and people emerged quickly. Tess showed neither surprise nor alarm, and after the melée had sorted itself out, she obeyed the instruction to lead onto the train. Becky stood on the entrance platform and dropped the handle of the harness so that Tess could relax for the short time it took the train to reach Bond Street station.

They made their way up into the bustle of Oxford Street where, as always, the traffic was heavy in both directions and there were crowds of people. This walk was a major test of Tess's ability to concentrate, for to her the road and pavements must have been a jumble of legs, shopping baskets, buses and taxis. She negotiated the street with no less skill than that demonstrated by

84

the humans, and with considerably more care than many pedestrians, who seemed to show a reckless disregard for their safety. When they crossed Oxford Street, Becky dropped the handle and took over, because no dog could be expected to avoid all the potential hazards. They went through the ground floor of one of the busy department stores, and Tess walked boldly and confidently, keeping alert and looking for the safest route through the forest of legs. There was no doubt that she was enjoying her work, and that she was for the most part fully in control.

The walk took just over half an hour, and the exercise was repeated with each dog. On the way back to Wokingham the instructors compared notes, and the general consensus was that it had been a valuable day's training for all the dogs, and that Tess was fast becoming the star pupil of the class.

Back at the centre, Dave Griffiths and his colleagues had another very important job to complete. It was now only about five weeks from the time that the dogs would complete their advanced training and be ready to meet their future owners, and all the dogs had to be carefully matched with the people on the waiting list.

Mary Townly had been on the list for almost a year. She had never had very good sight, and when she was thirteen it had failed completely. She had married when she was twenty-two, and with her husband's help had brought up their three children. They lived in a ground-floor flat about a hundred yards from Wandsworth Common in South London. Five years before, Jeff Townly had died tragically in a road accident, and Mary had managed to carry on on her own. Her elder son Rick was now twenty, and was a bus conductor with London Transport; her seventeen-year-old daughter Susan had just started work at the local supermarket and Mike, who was twelve, was still at school. Since Jeff's death, Mary had relied on the children and neighbours to help her with shopping and she enjoyed looking after their home. She had always been a very independent person, but the traffic in their neighbourhood was becoming so heavy that she was quite unable to get out and about on her own. She loved the open air and walking on the common, particularly around the ponds where she could hear the call of the coots and a colony of Canada geese had made their home. The fear of immobility seemed to be weakening her confidence, and she was determined to find a solution. She had heard about the Guide Dogs for the Blind Association, and it seemed to her that owning a guide dog would open a new life to her. It would be a challenge too, but she had surmounted so many problems over the years.

She talked the idea over with her children, and all three were enthusiastic about the idea, so Mary applied to the Association for a guide dog. She was visited by an instructor and after various formalities and questions it was agreed that Mary had the necessary physical and temperamental qualities to enable her to benefit from a guide dog, and she was placed on the list.

Mary's was one of the many case histories that Dave and his colleagues perused in matching the available dogs with the potential students. They had to make up twelve pairs for the final training course, and it had to be done well in advance so that should any student require a particular skill of the dog, like travelling to work by train, that could be given special attention during the remaining weeks of training.

On the list there were several people who needed dogs to replace the ones they already had, and they are always given priority. Some people had also expressed a preference for a particular breed or size of dog. Just because a name was at the top of the list did not mean that a person was first in line: the dogs had to match up with their owners. Far too much time and money was spent on the animals' training for them to be offered on a first-come, first-served basis.

Tess was paired with Mary Townly. The labrador had grown into a splendid animal, not too big, standing 20 inches at the shoulder. Her training was progressing well; she had shown that she was well suited to town work and that she would be able to cope with the hazards of a busy district of South London. Mary's flat was quite big enough to accommodate the animal, and Tess would get plenty of exercise on the common.

It took the instructors nearly three hours to complete a provisional list of twelve pairs and some reserves, and then the clerical staff took over the task of checking whether the students were available to attend the month-long residential course at the Wokingham centre.

Nine of the potential students accepted the invitation to go on the course, and Mary Townly was one of them. One man had to refuse because he was expecting to go into hospital, and two could not take any time off work, but another man had a much more understanding employer and had been granted paid leave to attend. Three of the "reserves" were able to accept, and the course was complete.

Now the work was intense. Tess's training with obstacles and traffic had to be reinforced; another dog had to spend more time in the country; two needed more practice at stations, and all had to work hard in traffic. The pairings were not sacrosanct: all sorts of things could change, but each dog was now being trained with a known recipient in mind. It was always possible that a dog might not take to its intended owner, and for that reason the instructors had to keep their arrangements flexible.

Mary out with her daughter Susan. She has had no mobility training, so the only way she can go out is when someone takes her out.

Much of Tess's obstacle work was done in the grounds of Folly Court on an artificially arranged course. There were obstacles under which she could easily pass, but which her handler could not, and there were obstacles which forced her to leave the kerb. She had to learn always to bring her handler back to the pavement after the obstacle was negotiated. She also spent a lot of time crossing and re-crossing roads in busy traffic, and the only times she had difficulty was when the "far" traffic came up too fast.

Soon, she was not failing in traffic at all. She was able to traverse busy areas like markets, and was taken to mingle in the crowds at the football ground in Reading. In the eighth week of her advanced training, her instructor started to work in a blindfold. It had to be done that way so that Becky could know how each dog would feel to a blind person and that the dog's skills could now be relied on. She did not expect any of the dogs to be able to lead her faultlessly at this stage, and there was always a colleague walking close at hand.

They went to all the places with which Tess was now familiar, and Becky became more and more confident of Tess's ability to concentrate. Some animals take advantage of the fact that their handlers cannot see what they are up to, but in the main Tess was very steady. Her instructor was able to relax in the knowledge that Tess was taking her full share of responsibility for their joint safety, and more. There was another trip in London, and once more Tess showed that she was an able pupil. The labrador had developed from a boisterous lively puppy into a mature and steady well-trained bitch. She still enjoyed her times for play, and was as nice a pet as one could hope to have, but when she was asked to work she responded with flair and genuine enthusiasm.

Now the only question was whether she and Mary Townly would make a successful pair.

CHAPTER THREE: Fulfilment

THE MONTH-LONG residential course at Wokingham started on a Friday. Three days before it began the dogs were seen by the vet, and unfortunately one of the german shepherds was found to have a heart condition and had to be rejected. That left the instructors with the sad task of informing one of the students that there would not after all be a place for him on the course, and so it was that eleven students assembled that Friday at Folly Court, in time for lunch.

The students had no contact with the animals that day. They spent the afternoon learning the layout of the centre, which is designed so that all the rooms the students use—bedrooms, dining room, common room, toilets, club room and bar and the animals' grooming room—are together in one part of the main building. The students have their own bedrooms, and the Association manages to provide excellent meals for only 90 pence per person a day.

Mary Townly was quite apprehensive. Although it was an informal first day, she found it quite difficult to adjust to the number of people there after her increasingly quiet life at home; many of the students would feel the same insecurity during the first few days.

That evening Dave Griffiths, the senior instructor on the course, gave the students an important lecture on various aspects of dog ownership, talking about the way dogs socialise and get to know their handlers, and explaining what would be required of them in grooming and feeding their dogs. He told them that there was a dog-bed in the corner of each student bedroom, and that the dogs should be encouraged to lie on it whether the student was with them or not. However they should keep the animals with them most of the time when they were moving about the building—in the past, some students had left the dogs in their rooms whenever they were not working, and that would help neither the dog nor its future owner. They were all welcomed to the centre and invited to make it feel like home—it was not an institution and anyone who felt like making a cup of coffee at three in the morning was welcome to do so.

Mary slept uneasily that first night. There had been so much to take in. She had been helped to learn the layout of the centre by the small braille notices on the doors, but the corridors were much longer and wider than any she had tackled recently. And there were her fears about her new dog. What kind

Short-harness work. Becky leads Mary to get her accustomed to the feel of the harness, before starting with the dog.

would it be? Would it like her? Would she be able to handle it properly? Had she made a dreadful mistake? She had visions of being dragged along an unknown roadway by some huge beast which she could not control. But eventually she slept, and by the morning she was ready to face the problem boldly. She knew that if she did fail it wouldn't be through lack of trying.

On the Saturday, the students began "short-handle work". No dogs were involved in this, so Tess and her kennel-mates had another day to themselves. Mary waited in the common room as the instructors took the first three trainees to work in the grounds. She got into conversation with another student, a Mr Pearce from Reading, who had come to get a replacement for his much-loved alsatian. He had had the alsatian for nine years, and it was ready for retirement. Fortunately his son and daughter-in-law were going to keep it as a pet, so they wouldn't be losing touch. (If the blind owner's relatives or friends cannot take over a retired guide dog, the Association arranges private homes for them.) After using a guide dog for so long Mr Pearce felt quite lost without one, and he hoped he was going to get on with

90

Tess watches Becky as she teaches Mary.

his new animal; there had been virtually no restrictions on his movements for nine years.

Mary learned a great deal from him. This mixing between the students is one important reason why the courses are residential; during the month they were together the students' confidence would grow because they would not be facing their problems on their own.

When it was Mary's turn, her instructor told her about the harness and handle which would be on the dog's shoulders, and the leash which would be around its neck. Mary took hold of the handle and lead as instructed in her left hand, and then, in the absence of the animal itself, the instructor took hold of the harness and held it at "dog height". This was "short-handle work"

Mary was taught the general commands to which the dog had been trained, and she learned also to gesture "forward" as she spoke the word. There was a lot of stopping and starting and this was why the dogs were not used on the first lesson. Even the best-trained dog in the world can get bored.

During that day, the students each had three training sessions, and by the evening had some idea of how it would feel to work with the dog in harness. Mary proved to be a quick learner, and the independence which David Pearce had described to her suddenly appeared within her grasp.

The students were asked whether they would prefer a night out at a local pub, or to relax in the bar at the centre, and the consensus was that an evening in would suit them all best. Mary used the time to good advantage, meeting more of her colleagues, and also talking to the resident guide dog owner Lorna, who managed to dispel any of the lingering doubts she had about her future with her dog. The party was in high spirits when the instructors interrupted to tell the students the names and breeds of the animals they were to have.

As Mary lay in bed that night, it wasn't fear that kept her awake. Tess. Now what was she? A yellow, no, a light yellow labrador. Honey-coloured. Mary could remember colours from her childhood. She wished the night away so that she could meet her dog.

On the Sunday morning, the students went into Wokingham in the mini-bus to continue their "short-handle" work. Being a Sunday, the town was fairly quiet, and there were few distractions for the students, who showed that for the most part they had absorbed the lessons of the previous day well. Then it was back to the centre and the meeting with the dogs.

They were told what to expect might happen when the dogs were introduced to them. The students were to make a fuss of the animals, but they were warned that the dogs might take more interest in the departing trainer than in them, and that they mustn't be discouraged by that. Then they returned to their own rooms to await the dogs' arrival.

Mary sat on her bed, her mind racing with the thought that she might not be able to cope, and when she heard the knock on the door she took a deep breath.

She heard the door open and the patter of the dog's paws as Tess was brought into the room.

"Here she is, Mary. This is Tess," said Becky. She removed Tess's lead and gave it to Mary, and left the room at once.

Having spent the past three days in kennels, Tess was in quite a boisterous mood, and she took very little notice of Mary, who tried to call her to her side without much success. Tess explored the room and tended to ignore Mary, but every so often they made contact. It was an awkward twenty minutes. Mary enjoyed the feel of Tess's coat, but it was some time before she could persuade her to come to sit beside her. Mary explored the labrador's shape with her hands, and managed to get her arms around the dog's neck for the

Tess and Mary meet.

occasional cuddle and Tess, who had always liked affection, responded with a wet lick at Mary's face. But if Mary had been hoping for an instant bond being formed between them she was out of luck, and it was obviously going to take time for them to get to know one another.

Similar meetings were taking place in the other rooms, and not all of them were easy. One lady, who had been on the waiting list for a long time because she was not very tall and needed a smallish dog, was overwhelmed with emotion on meeting her border collie. But in the main, the meetings went as well as could be expected, with more faults on the humans' side than the animals'; for both the students and the dogs this was the beginning of a new relationship.

They reassembled in the common room with their dogs, and most of the students managed to get there without the assistance of the vigilant instructors. They had been told that they should make their dogs "sit" if they stopped, to open a door for instance, and that if they stopped for longer they should get the dogs "down". Mary managed all right, except that she forgot to get the dog up again, and then nearly tripped over her. But she had another 25 days of practice to sort that out!

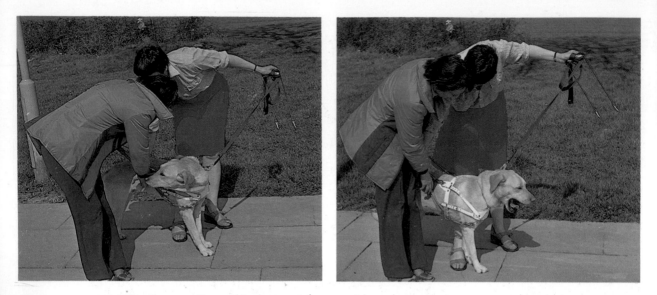

The first walk. Becky takes great care adjusting the harness—there are several different types of handle—so that Mary can feel exactly what Tess is doing. As they set off Becky takes the lead, while Mary has the harness. By the end of the first walk Mary was walking alone, holding both harness and lead.

Next, the students were taken two or three at a time to the grooming room. Mary would have to brush Tess every day, and she would feed her there as well, though on the first day the kennel staff would do it for her. On all subsequent days the food would be prepared in the kennels and left ready for the students to give the dogs. Mary would also be taught how to feel for any cuts or lumps on the dog's body, and to look for any symptons that might need the attention of a vet.

On Monday morning came the crucial first walk. Each student was taken to a quiet area close to Folly Court, where there were wide pavements free of obstacles. With the instructor holding the leash and Mary the harness handle, Tess took full control of the situation. All the hesitancy came from Mary, who was totally unused to being led in such a fashion. But because she had been blind for so long her stride was quite bold, and by the end of the walk she was beginning to enjoy the experience. At one point Mary felt she was being dragged to her left, but the watching instructor told her to trust the dog. Easier said than done, but confidence would come with time.

Back at the centre, the students who had completed their walks compared notes, and Mary realised that she was no less successful than any of the others, and there was much laughter as each recounted the things which had

94

gone wrong. And that was a feature of the course. The students refused to sit around despondently, and laughed at their mistakes. They investigated each other's dogs, and Mary soon found she could identify Tess from the group.

In the afternoon, Mary tried her hand at obedience with Tess in an enclosed run. She was fairly successful, but Tess needed a firm hand. Some dogs sense when a handler is physically unable to enforce a command, and some of the dogs "tried it on", but during the fifteen minute session Tess's response to Mary became quite good.

Mary was a good pupil, and her confidence began to build. She groomed and fed Tess, and by the time she went to bed she was feeling quite elated. It was a challenge, but not as alarming as she had feared and Tess, who was now curled up on her bed in the corner of the room, had already given her many moments of pure joy.

The training now intensified. Mary went out with Tess twice a day. At first she went on ordinary good-quality pavements with kerbs, but with few side

Practising "sit and stay" in class.

96

streets or obstructions, and again in fairly quiet areas. The aim was to maintain Tess's concentration and to increase Mary's. They performed lots of kerb approaches and step-off's, and Mary was taught to control Tess's speed. This was something she would have to do every time she went out with Tess, because a dog begins its walks fairly exuberantly, and that has to be curbed by consistent and firm control. Many didn't manage too well on that, but as her instructor said, it was "early days yet".

On the fourth walk, Mary was introduced to the concept of right and right-about turns. She managed these well from the start, and then they went into slightly busier areas where there would be a few shops, but not much traffic. The instructors also had to test that the dogs were truly responding to their new owners and not to them. This was done by telling the student that the instructor would be disappearing for a moment or two on the walk.

"My God, she's leaving me," thought Mary, the first time it happened, but so straight and even was Tess's pace that the instructor was back with them

Part of the group waiting their turn for instruction.

97

before Mary knew that the exercise had been attempted.

At the end of the first week, the students were given an appraisal of their work, and a further lecture on aspects of the training. It was impressed on them that the dogs had learned everything by repetition and consistency but that, although not everyone would agree, the dogs were capable of making decisions—they had been trained to disobey when necessary.

In the second week, Mary and Tess practised occasionally on an artificial obstacle course. There should have been no problem about Tess being able to negotiate the course, but on one occasion she was forgetful and tried to jump one of the low obstacles. But as there had been a lot of stopping and starting, Tess had got bored and had stopped concentrating. The bigger problem was whether Mary could follow the weaving animal and trust that it was doing the right thing. Mary had to learn to appreciate how much Tess was doing through her own sense of the environment, and how much she felt through the handle. Her instructor had a good idea of these feelings from working blindfold, and she was able to tell Mary how to interpret Tess's moves. They went on a full walk in the centre of Wokingham, and more than once Tess had to lead Mary off the kerb around an obstacle and then back on to the pavement. They managed the manouevre well, but a couple of other students found that instead of returning to the pavement they had been led across the road. That meant more work on the artificial obstacles in the grounds of Folly Court.

There was also the possibility that with a blind owner, the dog's ability to "read" traffic correctly would break down, and so the disobedience factor had to be reinforced in that second week. Mary was told to wrongly instruct the dog "forward" when she could hear it was not safe, frightening though this would be, because she had to test the dog's safety in traffic for herself. Tess didn't let Mary down, staying firmly put as the danger passed them by. Much praise was heaped on Tess, and Mary felt a growing affection for the well-trained labrador. There was no doubt that the bond between them was developing.

They had some sessions with "far" and "near" traffic work, and it was stressed to Mary that she had to help with this at all times. She must keep Tess alert in traffic, never allowing her to become less than efficient. Tess's concentration would be helped if Mary talked to her as much as possible although, as Dave pointed out, it was equally important that other people did not distract her—members of the public have to learn never to speak to a working guide dog.

There were moments of humour all the time. One of the students told his instructor that his dog was always lying on his bed rather than on its own,

Although Mary has given the command to go forward, Tess sits down as she can see the training car in the road.

On one of the group walks Mary and another student meet up with senior instructor Dave Griffiths who has been observing them.

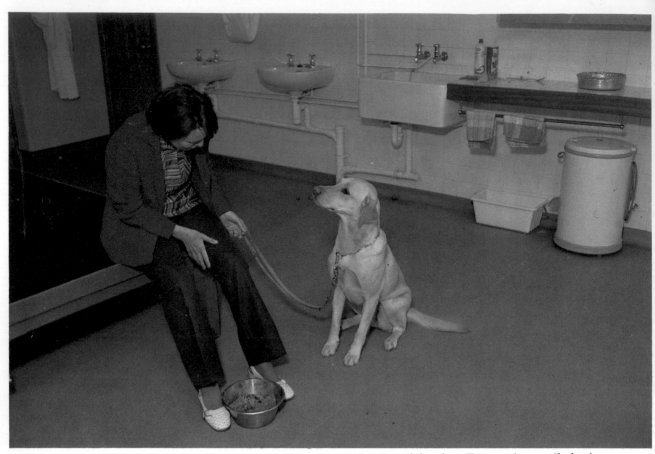

Food brings out the most spiritual expression in a labrador. Tess waits until she is given the go-ahead—

which was strictly against the rules. He was told to put a chair on the bed. The next time he came into the room the dog had climbed onto the chair and was fast asleep; the instructor pointed out that he had meant that the chair should be upside down!

Four of the students were having coffee in the common room with a visiting television crew. One of the dogs drank from a student's cup, which was on the floor, and the cameraman asked if the instructors would "turn a blind eye" to this lapse—there were gales of laughter from the students, who were not at all upset by the turn of phrase. The blind use the verb "to see" quite a lot—they talk of seeing a particular television programme, and on meeting someone will say "how nice to see you"—it's a word which causes no embarrassment at all.

The dining room is always entertaining. The students sit between the instructors and to begin with the dogs lie along the sides of the room, but during the last two weeks of training the students bring their dogs to lie quietly at their feet under the table.

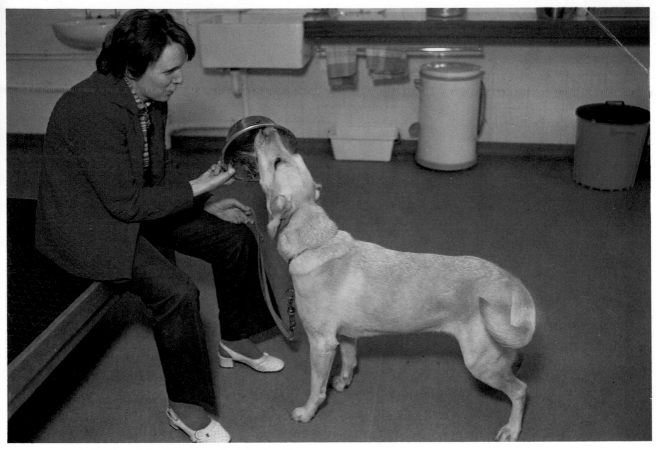

but the bowl is then emptied instantly.

The disability of blindness is not always treated too reverently. On one occasion when I was at Wokingham, a student walked across the main reception area with his dog on the leash but not in harness. He missed the way, and walked slowly into the window, to be told "Silly man," by Lorna, who from the reception desk had "seen" it all. Good humour abounds.

By the end of the second week, most of the students and their dogs had covered the basic work, and they could now go on without the trainer always being present as a secondary control. Most of the pairs were beginning to look good, and even the lady with the border collie seemed to have forgotten her fears.

The students were now taken to a fairly busy shopping centre. The general layout was explained to them and they were sent off down the street at two-minute intervals. This was a critical time, and although the instructors were not walking beside each student they were very close behind them, though dog and handler were unaware of that. Six students at a time were taken on these "group walks", and the instructors kept a careful watch as each unit of handler and dog negotiated the hazards in their path.

101

The walks have to be repeated endlessly to reinforce training. One day Tess gets very bored.

When they finally arrive back at Folly Court and have to go through the obstacle course, Tess forgets herself and is about to jump the barrier when at the last moment she thinks better of it. If a guidedog was born perfect it would not need to be trained.

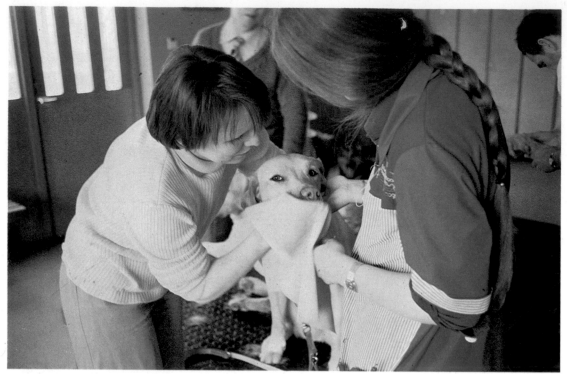

Learning to groom Tess.

Mary and Tess chatting to another student and his dog in a quiet moment at Folly Court.

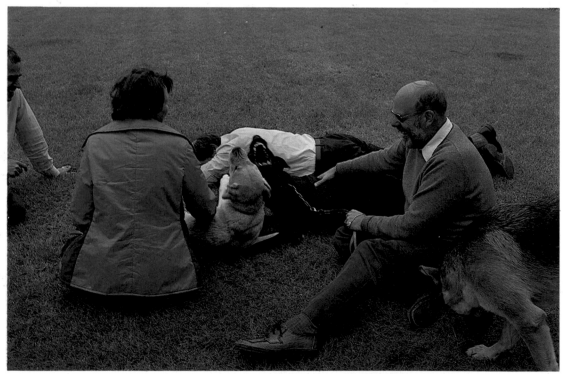

Although one might think Mike Cernovits' sheep in the grounds at Folly Court could be very distracting to dogs, Tess comes racing back to Mary's re-call, without a glance at the sheep.

Concentrated instruction in the centre of Reading . . .

They observed the dogs' kerb-sits, and how the students handled them. They watched for any dog taking liberties, and a couple behaved less well than they should have. At that point the instructors moved in, correcting the faults and making the students aware of the things they were doing wrong.

Tess and Mary managed the walk without too much difficulty, though Mary would later tell her family of the awful fear she had experienced on that first solo walk. Had she been able to see how well Tess worked with her, her fears would have been allayed.

The students later went on group walks through the centre of Reading. This involved all sorts of hazards, but the instructors had done their jobs well, and there were no mishaps. In fact, Mary and Tess did find themselves in difficulty at one of the main sets of traffic lights in the town. There was so much traffic that Mary was unable to work out the pattern of movement, and so reluctantly had to drop Tess's handle and wait for assistance. Her instructor was about to move in when an elderly gentleman stepped up to Mary and asked if he could help her. She gratefully accepted and took his arm

106

to be led over the junction. The man had obviously done this before—most people take hold of the blind person's arm and try to "steer" them, but this man allowed Mary to take *his* arm, in the correct manner.

Their route took them through crowds and into shops, past buses and into subways, and as usual there were some good laughs at the centre that night over incidents on the walk.

One man felt his instructor was bullying him, and he complained to Lorna about it. It turned out that his new labrador "did things differently" from his last one, and couldn't understand what he wanted.

"Well," said Lorna, "no two dogs are alike. You have to take each one from scratch, and learn about a new dog. It's easier for you to get to know this dog than for him to find out what your last one was like!"

He would remember what she had said the next day, and try to start a better relationship with his new dog.

Lenny, the big alsatian, was still distractedly looking for his instructor, and extra work was needed to help Mr Pearce establish his authority over the dog, and the lady with the border collie was having trouble too. She was not following the dog quite quickly enough after giving it an instruction.

. . . while Tess appears to be trying to hear what's said.

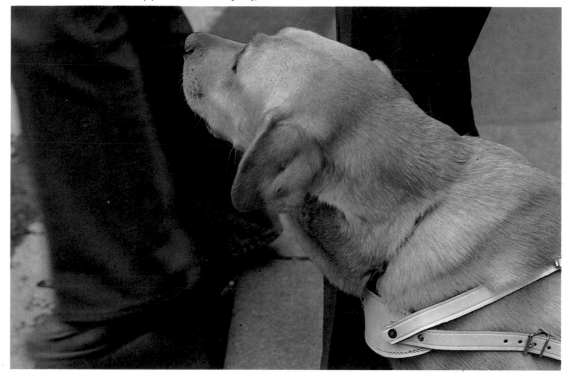

Tess leads Mary through streets full of obstacles in the centre of Reading, and off the train at Reading station.

It seemed that the animal's confidence was beginning to be affected, but when they all got talking together in the evening it seemed that almost any problem could be solved.

The bond between Mary and Tess was strengthening every day. They enjoyed their romps together in the run, and also the occasional trip to a wooded parkland nearby. There the dogs frolicked like any others, and made a great deal of noise, charging off into the undergrowth and bringing back sticks and branches. The fun would continue when the animals were re-called, and there were moments when two students tried to attach their leads to the same dog!

After a romp like that there was a lot of grooming to do. Dogs will always manage to get covered in mud if there is any around, and Tess was no exception. Luckily, Mary enjoyed cleaning her up—she loved the feel of her coat, the soft mouth and ever-cold nose, and she was so familiar with Tess's face by touch that she felt she could almost see it.

As the course continued, specialised training was given to the students who needed it. Of course there were difficulties in every pair, but the instructors were such highly skilled professionals that they could usually see a fault developing and correct it before the student was even aware that there was a problem.

The dogs are taken for a run in nearby woods. They are let off their leads one by one but have to wait until they're given the all clear—then they disappear like greased lightning—until they're recalled and come racing back.

Exercising the dogs is as important as the traffic training. The dog can't work well unless it has plenty of exercise to keep healthy. By this time Mary and Tess have a confident relationship—and Tess stays until she is allowed to join the other galloping dogs.

"Whose dog is this anyway!"

During each course the Guide Dog Association commissions a photographer to take pictures of the dog on its own to send to the breeder and puppy walker.

Relaxing after the photo session.

Tess meets Mary's children.

The Association believes it is important for the families and friends of the students to see the centre and discover how thorough the training is, and after two weeks there is a family visiting day. It is vital that training does not break down once the students and their dogs return home, and the chances of that happening are reduced if those who will be involved with the blind owners from day to day have first-hand experience of the work of the centre and see how the dogs are handled by the trainers.

So Mary's children came to meet Tess for the first time. As far as Mary was concerned, Tess was going to be her companion as well as her eyes, but to the family she would be first and foremost a welcome pet, and they took to her immediately. The day gave Mary a chance to talk to the children about her future, and the new freedom Tess would bring her. She could think positively about getting a job, and her sons and daughter were thrilled by her

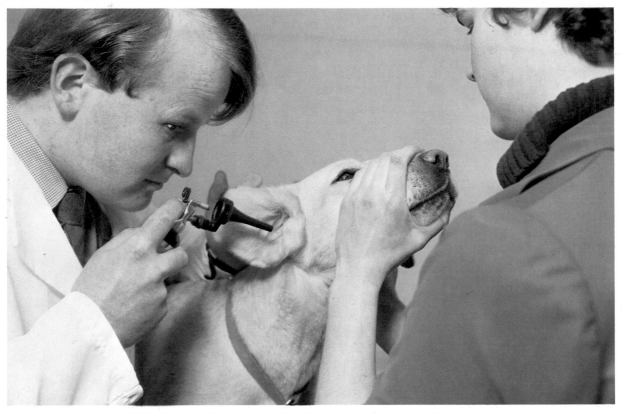

Before leaving Folly Court, Tess is given her final checkover by the Vet.

enthusiasm. One of the men on the course worked as a switchboard operator at a bank, and Mary realised that such work would not be beyond her. She could read braille, and Lorna had told her how easy she found typing. That was another possibility. Now that she could be mobile, she could be independent. She had not felt so optimistic for years, and it was the yellow labrador which was giving her confidence.

Brian Moody, the controller of the centre, and his assistant Mike Csernovits were well satisfied at the progress of the eleven pairs. They had been constantly on hand to help out with any problems experienced by either the students or the instructors, and now they were making plans for the arrival of the next group of students.

When the course entered its final week it was decided that the students had done so well that the training could be shortened by a few days, and this gave them further confidence.

119

An occasional "material reward" for a good dog.

Mary signs the contract to buy Tess for 50p

Two days before the end of the course came a most enjoyable formality. A buoyant Mary Townly entered Brian's office to enter into an agreement to buy Tess from the Guide Dogs for the Blind Association. The charge? A nominal 50 pence. As she signed the forms, Mary was elated. This was the fulfilment of a dream for her, and the moment of achievement for Tess too.

On the last night at Folly Court, the dogs were left in their new owners' rooms while the students and instructors had a celebration drink in the bar. As so often on the course, laughter predominated. The students had faced up to a new challenge and had won through to a new beginning, and the instructors had not only trained the dogs to their high level of ability but had helped the new owners to learn how to handle them. When the students dispersed from the centre the next day, each of them would be the owner of a skilled dog which would open the doors to a more independent life.

Tess and her new dog bed ready to go home.

Tess and Mary at home.

The story doesn't quite end there.

    Becky visited Mary and Tess the following Tuesday to see how they had settled in and to go over with Mary some of the routes she would expect to use more frequently. She checked the traffic light crossings and decided that with care they could all be negotiated without help; she thought Mary and Tess could manage even the junction on the South Circular Road because there was a pedestrian interval at the lights. She walked with them through the busy street-market in Northcote Road and was delighted to see the way they tackled it. Becky watched as Mary and Tess crossed Bolingbroke Grove, the busy road which formed a barrier between Mary's flat and the open delights of Wandsworth Common. They crossed—as Becky had known they would—with a confidence that many a sighted person would have envied.

Mary and her son Mike watch as Tess explores the garden.

Aftercare visit—Becky comes to advise Mary on the best routes round her area.

At last, Mary can go out independently with Tess.

Tess had come a long way from the tiny puppy which had to be persuaded to breathe to the fully grown bitch who was now capable of taking responsibility for Mary Townly's safety. Becky would continue to visit Mary and Tess regularly until they were completely established together. She was the last link in the chain which had begun with Derek Freeman and his assistants at the breeding centre eighteen months earlier and continued with Edith Washington and Alison Wallis, and with all the trainers and assistants who had been responsible for Tess at the Wokingham centre. It was a long chain, and in the end it had achieved its aim in giving a feeling of security and independence to one more blind human.

Tess is a guide dog.

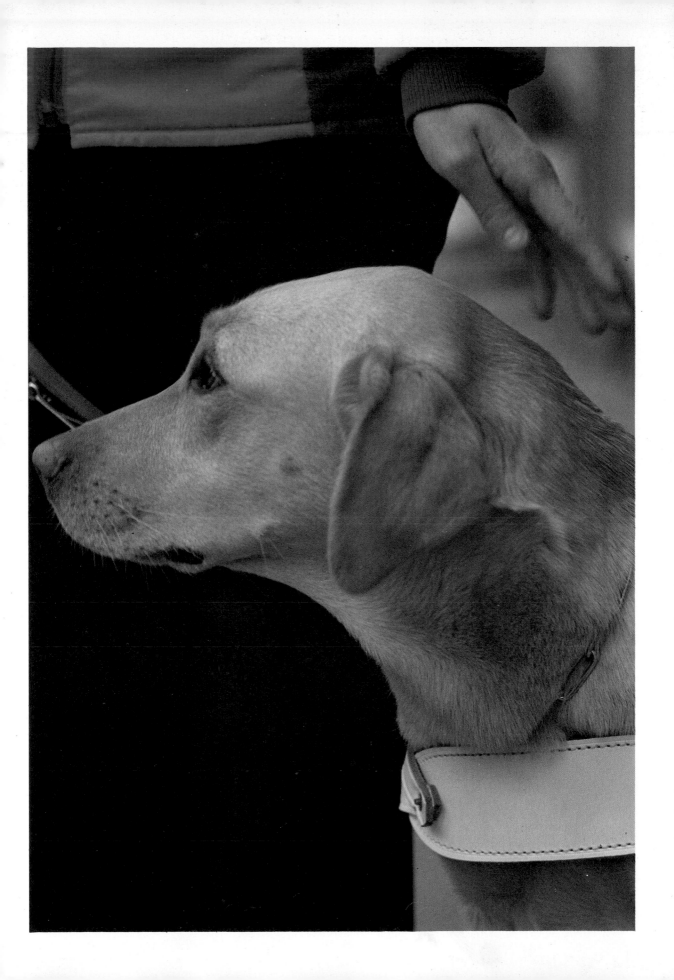

Epilogue

IN EVERY TOWN in Britain, guide dogs can be seen leading their sightless owners. Each one has been trained to the same high standards Tess attained, and each one is a tribute to the care and devotion of the staff of the Guide Dogs for the Blind Association. Without them, many hundreds of blind people would be less able to cope with the increasing difficulties of modern life. The dogs are not born special, but their training makes them exceptional. They are the eyes of the blind.

Tess is typical though she does not really exist: she is an amalgamation of many dogs trained by the GDBA each year. Mary Townly is a fictional person too, but her life and problems are not unlike those of many blind people who seek the help of a guide dog. Edith Washington and her family are also fictional, but they are an example of the helpers without whom the work of the Association could not even begin. We are grateful to the real Mary and Edith for their cooperation in preparing this book.

Derek Freeman, Barrie Stocks, Alison Wallis, Brian Moody, Mike Csernovits, Dave Griffiths, Lesley Malcolm and Becky Oldfield all do the jobs described, and we would like to thank them, and Alan Brooks, for their considerable help.

London, 1981

F.G.
P.P.

126

A Short History

THE METHODICAL TRAINING of dogs to guide the blind began in Germany in 1916, when a doctor in charge of a clinic for the war-wounded was called away from a blind man with whom he was walking in the grounds, and left his alsatian to look after the patient. He was so impressed with the response that he began to train dogs to lead the blind.

In 1927, Mrs Harrison Eustis, the American founder of the Fortunate Fields kennels at Mount Pelerin, Switzerland, where alsatians were trained for the army, customs service and police, visited the guide dog training centre in Potsdam. She wrote an article about it in the *Saturday Evening Post*, and among the letters she received was one from Morris Frank, asking if she could train a guide dog for him. In 1928 he became the first American to own a trained guide dog. Mrs Eustis set up a school in Switzerland called L'Oeil qui voit—the Seeing Eye—for training guide dogs and their blind owners, and later established the Seeing Eye in the United States.

An account of her work in the British press in 1930 prompted a Mr Robert Tissyman to write to the *Liverpool Echo* asking anyone interested in training guide dogs to contact Mr Musgrave Frankland, Liverpool secretary of the National Institute for the Blind. Miss Muriel Crooke, a trainer living in Wallasey, near Liverpool, and Mrs Rosamund Bond, a breeder and exhibitor of alsatians, were two who responded, and although Mr Frankland had known nothing of the original appeal he gave the project his enthusiastic support. A committee was formed to set up a pilot scheme, and Mrs Eustis advised them; training could only be done by a qualified instructor, and near a town. The committee managed to raise over £284, and became affiliated to the National Institute for the Blind.

The training of guide dogs in Britain began in 1931 on a piece of rented open ground near Miss Crooke's home in Wallasey, with a lock-up garage for use as a dog room and store. Mrs Eustis lent the services of a trainer from her school, and there were seven alsatian bitches on the first training scheme. Four of the five blind men accepted as students emerged as successful guide dogs owners, and a further four men were trained the following year. An appeal on the BBC in 1933 brought in donations of over £750, and the Association was now able to find better premises and engage a permanent trainer. Captain Nikolai Liakhoff, a former officer of the Russian Imperial Guard and a member of Mrs Eustis's staff, arrived in October 1933. Conditions improved when The Cliff, a rambling house close to the seashore, was acquired from Wallasey Corporation at a very low rent. Work continued there until the war, when the house was requisitioned as an anti-aircraft battery and later destroyed by bombing. In 1941 the Association was able to purchase Edmonscote Manor near Leamington Spa. Here Captain Liakhoff and his wife managed to get kennels built and establish a permanent training centre.

In 1951 a second training centre was opened in Exeter, and the first purpose-built centre began operating in Bolton in 1961. A fourth centre opened in Forfar, Scotland, in 1965, and the fifth in Wokingham, Berkshire, in 1977. The GDBA plans to build a sixth training centre in the northeast of England to open in 1982. A breeding scheme was started in the early 1960s and has its own premises at Tollgate House, near Warwick; it now provides most of the Association's puppies.

The guide dog movement is well-established in many countries, including Australia, New Zealand, South Africa, France, Germany, Switzerland, Holland, Italy, the Scandinavian countries, the United States and Canada. Through the help of guide dogs, thousands of blind people have been able to acquire independence and mobility.

There are about 2,800 working guide dogs in Britain and some five hundred new dogs are trained each year. Nearly half of these go to existing guide dog owners as replacements. Despite the growth of training facilities, demand still exceeds supply, and there is a waiting list for places at the training centres.

A guide dog is trained for seven or eight months before being paired with a blind student. Then there are a further four weeks of residential training while the dog and its future owner learn to work together safely. All this, together with the breeding and aftercare programmes, is very expensive, but it has always been a basic principle that lack of money should not prevent a blind person from owning a guide dog, and so a nominal charge of only fifty pence is made for the guide dog.

The Guide Dogs for the Blind Association receives no financial aid from the state, and the generosity and goodwill of the public are therefore essential to enable it to continue its work. It you would like to help, the head office will be happy to send you further information; contact
The Guide Dogs for the Blind Association,
Alexandra House,
9/11 Park Street,
Windsor,
Berkshire SL4 1JR,
England.